HINDU POLITICAL THOUGHT

HINDU POLITICAL THOUGHT

BY

AJIT KUMAR SEN

Gian Publishing House

29/6 SHAKTI NAGAR · DELHI-110007 · INDIA

GIAN PUBLISHING HOUSE
PUBLISHERS OF BOOKS ON HUMAN CIVILIZATION
29/6 SHAKTI NAGAR, DELHI-110007

First Reprint in India, 1986

Printed at Goyal Offset Printers, Delhi-110035
and published by Smt. Gayatri Garg
for Gian Publishing House, Delhi-110007

PREFACE

In one sense, it was an evil day for India when the *Sacred Books of the East* made their appearance: it showed to what absurd lengths 'other-worldliness' could go. That the culture of the ancient Hindus was a well-balanced one and that they were as much worldly as any other people, have been amply demonstrated by recent researches in Indology. The present book is the outcome of a desire to establish the fact, that in realms of political thought, the Hindus were not as backward as some writers try to make out; and with that end in view, I have examined some aspects of political thought in some detail.

Most of the articles incorporated in this book were originally meant for periodicals: this will, perhaps, explain the manner of treatment and some unavoidable repetitions which have crept into the book. I have throughout dealt with political thought, and have no concern with political institutions as such. I had a mind to make the book more comprehensive by including some more articles in it, dealing with the nature of punishment, ideal of universal sovereignty etc.; but for some reason I had to give up the idea. Up till now, the literature on the subject is scanty, though growing, and it requires many serious students to explore it in full: it is with this end in view, and also to facilitate comparative study, that ample footnotes have been added.

I have to thank the editors of the *Calcutta Review* and the *Modern Review* for their kindness in allowing me to incorporate some articles which appeared in their Reviews. (I) and (VII) appeared in the former in four issues,—March, 1925 ; Sept., Nov., Dec., 1925 —while (V) appeared in the latter in Oct., 1924.

To my former teacher Sj. Satis Chandra Ray one cannot be too highly grateful : it was he, who, in the beginning, encouraged me in my contributions to the periodicals. It is both a pleasure and duty to acknowledge my indebtedness to the writings of Professors Benoy Kumar Sarkar and Upendra Nath Ghoshal and to those of Dr. Pramatha Nath Banerjee ; specially so, in the case of my article on the origin of kingship. My colleague, Sj. Jyotirmoy Sen of the Dacca University, has occasionally helped me with suggestions, while Sj. Sarat Chandra Sen and my brother Sm. Abani Kumar Sen have considerably lightened my labours by helping me in revising the proofs.

AJIT KUMAR SEN

I. RAGHUNATH CHATTERJEE STREET
CALCUTTA

June 7, 1926

CONTENTS

IS HINDU POLITICS THEOLOGICAL

"THE Oriental Aryans never freed their politics from the theological and metaphysical environment in which it is embedded to-day." This opinion, coming as it does from Professor Dunning(*a*), requires to be carefully and seriously examined.

The implication of Prof. Dunning's statement is that politics as such had no independent status, that it was always tied to the apron-strings of religion and metaphysics :and that the ancient Hindus, unlike the Greeks, were perfectly innocent of politics as a distinct branch of learning.

Let us first of all consider the various forms of classification of sciences and arts as known to the ancient Hindus. As tradition has it, the primary *vidyas* or sciences are thirty-two in number, the primary *kalas* or arts being sixty-four(*b*). And of the thirty-two sciences(*c*) Arthasastra is one. But according to Sukracharya, Arthasastra is a two-fold science(*d*), *viz.*, Politics as well as Economics. But

(*a*) *History of Pol. Theories, Ancient and Mediaeval*, Intro. xix.

(*b*) *Sukraniti*, IV-III, 46 (S.B.H. Vol. 13).

(*c*) The distinction between science and art is almost the same as that between Vidya and Kala.

(*d*) IV-III, 110-11, but see Ghoshal's "*Hindu Pol. Theories*," p. 129.

in pre-Kautilyan ages Politics had been sharply differentiated from Economics—the two other sciences being Anvikshaki and Trayi. The school of Manu held that there were only three sciences, *viz.*, Trayi, Vartta (Economics) and Dandaniti (Politics); the school of Brihaspati opined that Vartta and Dandaniti were the only two sciences that counted. The school of Usanas declared that politics was the only science and it was in this science that all other sciences had their origin and end(*a*). With the exception of Sukracharya's conception of Arthasastra, which includes the sciences of Economics and Politics, all the other classifications treat Politics as independent of Trayi and Anvikshaki, *i.e.*, independent of theology and metaphysics. Sukra gives a list of 32 sciences, and it is remarkable that the doctrines of Nastikas (sceptics), Arthasastra and Kamasastra are as much distinct branches of learning as Samkhya, Vedanta and the various Vedas. If this *Nastika Vidya* which advocates the predominance of Reason and denies the existence of Vedas and ascribes the origin of all things to Nature and not to God(*b*), can be held as a distinct branch of learning even by the "wholly religious-minded" (a misnomer no doubt) Hindus, it is difficult, in these circumstances, to appreciate the opinions of those scholars who would call Hindu Politics theological and metaphysical(*c*). Not that

(*a*) *Kautilya*, I,2.

(*b*) *Sukra*, IV-III, 108-9.

(*c*) How far religious ideas influenced the polity of the Hindus has been described by Dr. Narendra Law in his "*Aspects of Ancient Indian Polity,*" ch. 9; but he has

some systems—if systems they can be called—of Hindu politics are free from theological or metaphysical taints—but it would be wrong, nay positively untrue, to say that Hindu politics as a whole is theological, *i.e.*, the Hindus could not conceive of positive politics. When Nastika Vidya and Kamasastra and other ultra-secular vidyas can be conceived of as distinct branches of learning, it is difficult to see why Arthasastra should be denied an honourable and distinct place in the list of sciences and arts.

According to pre-Kautilyan tradition Politics ranked with Vedas and Anvikshaki as an independent science ; but when we come to Brihaspati, we come across a remarkable classification of sciences, in as much as only two positive and social sciences are given the appellation of science—the rest being deemed negligible or subordinate. It was reserved for Usanas to declare that Politics is *the* science —all other sciences being included within it(*a*).

Critics may point out that this classification which ascribes to politics the character of an

been careful to add that "the religious aspects of polity summed up in this chapter**should not be mistaken for the whole of polity but are mere aspects" (p. 218).

(*a*) We might, in this connection, recall Aristotle's conception of Politics. Considered from the abstract standpoint, Politics included ethics, though practically he separated the two. As the Greeks could not conceive of anything except in and through the state, it is but reasonable to assume that to the Greeks and to Aristotle politics is the dominant, "architectonic" science. But Aristotle himself often confused the respective spheres of politics and ethics. As a matter of fact it is difficult to completely separate the two, because in all social sciences, standards and norms are sure to come in. See Dunning, *Pol. Theories, Ancient*, pp. 51-54.

independent branch of learning may prove something but not all. That is true, but the importance of the fact of Nastika-vidya being placed along with the Vedas, should not be lost sight of. This raises a presumption, and nothing more is intended, that politics might as well be a secular and positive science(*a*). But Brihaspati and Usanas even went so far as to declare that theology (Trayi) and metaphysics (Anvikshaki) are not independent sciences,—which implies the extreme secularization of politics.

Next we come to the point that some authoritative Hindu writers of Politics, at least, treated Politics from the positive point of view. A study of Kautilya's Arthasastra leaves no doubt in one's mind, that the whole book is written from a positive and secular standpoint. In a striking passage (IX, 4) Kautilya inculcates the doctrine of the superiority of human effort over fate and pertinently remarks that wealth will certainly pass away from an idiot who consults the stars too much ; for wealth is the star of wealth and the stars in the sky have nothing to do with it. Kautilya even goes so far as to say that the course of the progress of the world depends on the science of Dandaniti(*b*). This means that nothing is pre-

(*a*) *Cf.* "It is however a remarkable fact that the study of statecraft*** might be called a secular science, were it not for the pronounced disinclination of the Hindu mind to conceive the secular life as the antithesis of the religious."—Ghoshal's '*Hindu Political Theories,*' Preface ix. To the Hindus the concept Dharma implies an admixture of socio-ethico-religious ideas—not a purely religious concept.

(*b*) *Kautilya*, I,4.

ordained, man can shape the future course of the world with the help of Dandaniti. This emphasis on the positive and secular aspect of Politics is remarkable because of the fact that this view-point was enunciated not in the 20th century but more than 20 centuries ago(*a*).

Sukra was more emphatic on this point. His enunciation of the doctrine of *Puruskara* might, as well and with good grace, have come from modern writers who believe in the doctrine of the 'open future.' Sukra says that the king is the cause or maker of time(*b*), that man's work is the cause of his good or bad luck(*c*), that wise men respect Paurusa or Energy, whereas the weaklings worship Daiva or Fate(*d*), that the king is the cause of the prosperity of this world(*e*), that the faults are to be ascribed neither to the age nor to the subjects but to the king(*f*). The dictum of Sukra (IV-V 525-8) that human evidence ought to be preferred to a divine one also goes to support the secular character of the science. Now all this involves a positive conception of politics—untainted by theological and metaphysical

(*a*) The fact that Kautilya—the minister of Chandra Gupta Maurjya—himself laid the foundation of a well-organized extensive empire by dint of his own exertions, may serve to explain the emphasis which Kautilya laid on the positive aspect of Politics.

(*b*) I, 43-4, 119-20 ; IV-I, 116-7.

(*c*) I, 73-4.

(*d*) I, 95-6. See *Matsya Purana*, Ch. 221 (S.B.H., Vol. 17, Part II) and *Kamandakaniti*, XIV, 21.

(*e*) I, 127-8.

(*f*) IV-I, 116-7.

considerations(*a*). In the Mahabharat also Bhisma expresses the view that the king is the cause of time, not *vice-versa*—that the king is the creator of the four ages. In the Mahabharat the origin of kingship is both popular and divine, which means that secular politics and canonical politics got blended together. Sometimes these two schools remained separate, sometimes they approached each other and again sometimes they intermingled(*b*). But the fact should not be lost sight of that there was a positive background in almost all the political speculation in the Santiparva(*c*). Here and there theological hues appear, but they never overwhelm the positive and secular background. The state of nature so vividly described in the Mahabharat and so strongly resembling that painted by the

(*a*) Some theological taint may be discovered in Sukra's conception of the origin of kingship (I, 375), but here we get a blend of secular and canonical politics. In Sukra we rarely meet with canonical ideas of politics. See my article, 'The Arthasastra of K. and the Nitisastra of S.'

(*b*) On this point, Upendranath Ghoshal's "*Brahminical Conception of the Science of Politics*" in *Sir A. Mookerjee Jubilee Volumes* (*Orientalia* I) may be of some help. It is possible as Rai Bahadur Srish Basu opines (see his *Intro. to Yagnabalka Smriti* in S.B.H., Vol. 21) that in course of time the Smriti writers incorporated whole sections of politics written by the secular school. A guess may be hazarded that when the Hindus lost their political supremacy—they incorporated portions of Arthasastra (secular politics) in their sacred laws and thus carried on the village government without coming into contact with the conquerors.

(*c*) It should be noted that Bhisma in his lectures to Yudhisthira made a significant admission when he said in effect that Rajadharma, as he conceived it, is not based on canonical writings only but also on reason and experience.

"contract school"—the election of kings, the coronation-oath of Prithu—do not these things suggest the positive and secular character of Santiparva Politics ? Moreover, deposition and tyrannicide are only sanctioned when kings are "men" and politics secularized,—and Mahabharat sanctions them.

The conception of Law is one of the touchstones whereby the secular and positive character of politics can be ascertained. There is an impression abroad that Hindu writers on Politics had no conception of Positive Law. The only conception of law they possessed had its origin and sanction, it is said, in religious scriptures (*a*). It will be idle to deny that some writers seek the sanction in scriptures ; but it will be untrue to say that no Hindu writer on politics had any conception of positive law as it is understood to-day. By positive laws, we mean laws enforced by a sovereign political authority(*b*).

Now if we turn for a while to Sukra, we shall see that Sukra has a clear notion of what positive law is. Sukra says, "The following laws are to be always promulgated by the king among his subjects" and then says that falsehoods must not be practised with regard to weights and measurements, currency, etc. ;

(*a*) Willoughby, *Nature of the State*, p. 12.—We might recall here the Greek conception of 'revealed' laws and the part played by the Delphic Oracle. For a fuller study see my article, 'The Concept of Law and the Early Hindu View.'

(*b*) Holland, *Jurisprudence*, Ch. IV ; actual instances of positive law may be seen in Aiyangar's *Ancient India* (Chola Adm). Some of Asoka's edicts are in the nature of positive law. See Benoy Sarkar's *Pol. Institutions* etc Ch. 4. Sec. 5.

that bribes must not be accepted ; that thieves must not be given protection ; that tanks, wells, parks must not be obstructed ; that without proper licenses gambling and hunting must not be practised and so forth and that those who after hearing these laws promulgated, act contrary to them, will be severely punished by the king (*a*). All the requisites of positive law are present in Sukra's doctrine, namely, a sovereign political authority, clearly promulgated laws and punishment by the king in the event of disobedience to laws(*b*).

The Santiparva of Mahabharat though not so clear on the point, describes three kinds of Vyabahara or Law ; one of which, arising out of the disputes of the litigants, inheres in the king. Kautilya in his *Arthasastra* distinguishes four kinds of law, *viz.*, *Dharma* (sacred law), *Vyabahara* (evidence), *Charitra* (custom) and *Rajasasana* (edicts of king)(*c*). Had Kautilya said nothing further, we would have been justified in assuming that Kautilya's political authority was not legally sovereign. But later on(*d*) Kautilya says, "whenever there is disagreement between history (custom) and sacred law or between evidence and sacred law, then the matter shall be settled in accor-

(*a*) *Sukraniti*, I, 603-24. For some instances of positive municipal law see *Indian Antiquary* 1905 pp. 51-2.

(*b*) Holland writes thus in the Chap. on "Positive Laws"—"A law as carried by Pericles, or as imagined by Plato, would conform to Austin's definition as completely as would a constitution of Marcus Aurelius." In the place of "Plato" Holland might have substituted the name of Sukra and the sense would be unaltered.

(*c*) *Artha*, III, 1. (*d*) *Ibid*.

dance with sacred law. But whenever sacred law is in conflict with rational law (king's law), then reason shall be held authoritative; for there the original text (on which the sacred law has been based) is not available." It clearly suggests that the king is the sovereign law-making power. The legalisation by royal decree of Charudatta's marriage with Vasantasena depicted in the Mricchakatika shows the superiority of king's law to sacred law.

To Narada legalism is everything—even ethical judgments are not allowed to encroach on the sacred preserves of law. "Whatever a king does is right, that is the settled rule(*a*),"—is a dictum which may frighten away the modern jurists. "As a husband, though feeble, must be constantly worshipped by his wives, in the same way a ruler though worthless must be (constantly) worshipped by his subjects(*b*)." We doubt if even the most ardent advocates of the Prussian theory of state would let such a dictum pass unchallenged.

An Act of Indemnity passed by the British Parliament is the greatest proof of its legal sovereignty, for it legalises illegality(*c*). Is not the

(*a*) *Narada,* XVIII, 21. On the alleged influence of Equity in Hindu Jurisprudence see an article by Jayaswal in the *Cal. Weekly Notes,* Vol. 15, entitled, "Origin of Equity in Hindu Jurisprudence."

(*b*) *Ibid,* XVIII, 22—compare the following from *Calvin's Institutes.* Bk. IV, Ch. XX, para. 25:—Even an individual of the worst character, one most unworthy of all honour, if invested with public authority * * * * in so far as public obedience is concerned, he is to be held in the same honour and reverence as the best of kings. (Quoted by *Dunning*).

(*c*) *Dicey's Law of the Constitution,* p. 233, 8th edition.

same legalisation of illegality evident when Narada asks, "How should a king be inferior to a deity, as it is through his word that *an offender may become innocent* and an innocent man an offender in due course(*a*)." So much for the argument that Narada had a true conception of positive law as it is understood by the analytical school of jurists. That he also had a secular conception of society, and hence political society, may be inferred from his sloka(*b*) where he lays down that *Vyabahara* is superior to *Dharma*, and reason(*c*) is to be laid under obligation as a source of law, when there is a conflict with the Dharmasastras(*d*). If by *Vyabahara* we mean customs, then in a conflict of customs with *Dharma* the latter is to go to the wall ; and evidently here customs mean secular customs, otherwise *Dharma* would not have been ignored by Narada. Again, if by *Vyabahara*, the *Vyabahara* portions of the *Smritis* are meant, then it comes to this that in a conflict between the two portions of the *Smritis, viz., Vyabahara* and *Dharma*—the former is to prevail(*e*). Whatever

(*a*) *Narada*, S.B.E., XVIII, 52. Charudatta's marriage with Vasantasena in the Mricchakatika is an instance to the point. See *Calcutta Weekly Notes*, Vol. 16. pp ii-ix.

(*b*) *Narada* I,40.

(*c*) Evidently the reason of the king is implied since there may be further conflict between reasoned opinions of various individuals. Hobbes in his Leviathan impatiently enquires as to whose reason is to hold good and answers by saying that king's reason is to hold good on the ground that otherwise there would be no end of conflicts of opinion.

(*d*) *Cf. Kautilya Artha.*, III, 1.

(*e*) But Yagnabalka says—Arthasastra is inferior to Dharmasastra in authority. II, 21.

interpretation is accepted, it will be seen that Narada has a distinct leaning towards the secular side, though it must not be forgotten that the Hindu mind cannot conceive the attribute 'secular' as distinctly antithetical to the attribute 'religious.'

We can now see that the conception of law rises layer by layer till it reaches the heights of Narada's pure rationalistic legalism. It is 'legalism', because Narada would not allow any extraneous or ethical considerations to come in; and it is rationalistic, because in reason's conflict with authoritative canonical laws, the latter are to be ignored. And whenever reason is extolled over sacred authority, or for the matter of that, any authority, it is clear, that a secular conception of law and hence of politics, is implied. The conception of law in the *Santiparva* denotes the first stage, the next stage is reached by Sukracharjya, Kautilya carries it a stage higher until we come to Narada's, which is ultra-modern in its nature(*a*).

Some theories about the origin of kingship go to emphasize the secular aspect of political thought. The Vedic kings were mere mortals and as such often deposed and expelled(*b*). Whether the subjects elected their kings as Zimmer says, or selected by the people from among the members of the royal family as Macdonell implicitly assumes(*c*), does not affect our argument, in as much as both of them admit, that in the matter of origin of kingship, some popular

(*a*) No corresponding chronology is implied, but only the development in the order of thought.

(*b*) S.B.E., Vol. XLIV, p. 269.

(*c*) *Vedic Index*, Vol. II, p. 211.

element at least is involved—and that is sufficient(*a*). The dictum of *Baudhayana* that the king is to get the revenue not as a matter of right, but as his salary for protecting the subjects(*b*), underlies almost all the theories of kingship in the Buddhist and Brahmanic canons and the implication of this dictum is evident.

In the Ramayana and the Mahabbharat, no doubt, we often come across contrary theories ; but we must not overlook the fact that both the epics distinguished tyrants from good kings—a distinction carefully maintained by Sukra. Both the epics give no quarter to a tyrant, and in Ramayana it is said, that a king who is unkingly is no king, and therefore no God, and hence could be killed like a mad dog(*c*). The Mahabbharat is equally emphatic on the point(*d*). We also find that "Atri was the first to deify a king, so that Gautama called him a sycophant, but Sanatkumara upheld the deification(*e*)." The implication is that Gautama opposed the deification of kings—

(*a*) Of course later Vedic Literature begins to hint divinity to kings. "And as to why a Rajanya shoots. he, the Rajanya, is manifestly of Prajapati : hence while being one, he rules over many"—Satapatha-Brahmana V. I. 5, 14. *Cf.* "This much is certain that neither during the Vedic period nor in the times of Kautilya divine birth or right of kings seems to have been thought of." Shamasastri, *Evolution of Indian Polity*. p. 145.

(*b*) I. 10, 1 ; see *Sukraniti* (S.B.H., Vol. 13) I, 375.

(*c*) Quoted from Hopkins' *Epic Mythology*, p. 64. See *Indian Historical Quarterly*, Vol. I. No 3, pp. 495-6.

(*d*) Bhisma quotes Rishi Bamdeva, *Santiparva*, Section 92. See the Vena story. In the Anusasana Parva subjects are advised to arm themselves for slaying a tyrant. Sukra sanctions deposition of tyrants. See II, 549-52.

(*e*) *Epic Mythology* by Hopkins, p 184.

which means, that to Gautama at least, the institution of kingship was secular and human. Even when hereditary kingship is in vogue, the tradition of election is kept up, as is evident from the Mahabharat(*a*). The theories of the origin of kingship as described in the Mahabharat are both popular and divine, and hence involve a blend of secular and non-secular conceptions.

The theory about the origin of kingship as described in the *Dighanikaya*(*b*), goes to show the secular character of political thought in a very clear and definite manner. Here at first a blissful state of nature, as described by Rousseau, is followed by degeneration(*c*), wherefore people assemble together to choose one as their king. This king is known as the Mahasammata(*d*). In the Jatakas we come across many instances of election of kings by councillors or people (*e*). This principle of election is carried to such a great extent, that fish and birds are

(*a*) Hopkins' article in *J. A. O. S.*, 1889. See also Jayaswal's chapters on Coronation in *Hindu Polity*.

(*b*) *Aganna-suttanta*, *Dighanikaya—Cf.* Aryadeva's view.

(*c*) In the Mahabharat there are two accounts. (1) Anarchy to be followed by the creation of a state, (2) Blissful state followed by anarchy—the latter followed by the birth of a state.

(*d*) A similar elective origin of kingship is to be found in the Tibetan *Dulva* translated by Rockhill. In the Brahmanas we come across elective origin of Indra's kingship. In Ait. Brah. there is a passage relating to the election of kings by the Devas ; the election being the result of the stress of war between the Devas and the Asuras.

(*e*) VI, 462 ; II, 270.

depicted as choosing their respective kings(*a*). The implications of the contractual origin of kingship are far-reaching, but it is to be regretted that such theories were not followed by systematic theories about the rights of people. Possibly Hindu political thought delighted in laying more stress on Swadharma (duties) than on Swadhikara (rights). Whatever be the reason, there can be no doubt, that people, as depicted in the Jatakas, understood the implications of the contract theory and were not slow to take advantage of them as will be evident from some of the Jataka stories(*b*). There we find subjects expelling a king for developing cannibalistic propensities, and even killing one for rank ingratitude and all this would not have been common, had the people deified their kings(*c*).

(*a*) II, 270. See the account where one bird proposes owl's name ; another opposes because of owl's owlish face. Finally a golden goose is elected.

(*b*) *Saccamkira Jat.*, Vol. I; *Padakusalamanava Jat.*, Vol. III; *Mahasuttasoma Jat.*, Vol. V (Cowell's Edition).

(*c*) Sukra's king must have god-like attributes—otherwise he would be turned out. See I, 141-3, 139-40, 363-4. The ruler, according to Sukra, has been made a *servant* of the people by the *Brahma* getting his revenue as his wages. A blend of secular and canonical idea no doubt, but one who runs may perceive that Sukra's conception of nitisastra is emphatically secular and positive.

For some theories about kingship in ancient India see an article entitled, "Kingship in Ancient India" in the *Journal of the Bihar and Orissa Research Society*, 1920, Volume VI, by J. Samaddar. For an admirable criticism of Jayaswal's views see *Indian Hist. Quarterly* Vol. I. No. 2, pp. 378-84. In connection with deification of kings it may be added that Buddhism with its agnosticism cannot sanction divine origin or rights of kings. The later Brahmanic conception of divine kings was necessitated by the fact—so Shamasastri says (p. 146, *Evo. of Ind. Polity*)—of "hiding the low birth of restored Dravidian kings of the

Thus, whether we look at the question from the point of view of classification, or doctrine of Puruskara or conception of law or the theory of kingship, it is evident that Hindu political thought properly so-called—is not theological but predominantly secular and positive.

Buddhist period and of strengthening their royal power so as to be able to guard the interest of the Brahmanas."

SCOPE AND NATURE OF HINDU POLITICAL LITERATURE

THE *rajadharma* sections of the Dharmasutras and the Dharmasastras represent one type of Hindu political thought, while the other type is fairly represented by the Arthasastras and the Nitisastras. Hindu political thought, no doubt, had its origin in the Vedic literature and developed to a certain extent in the Dharmasastras ; but only as an appendage : it was only in the hands of the Arthasastric school that political thought came to its own and claimed an independent status. In the Dharmasastras of an earlier age politics received a step-motherly treatment and even in a later period there were canonists (e.g. Yagnabalka) who would have politics go to the wall if and when, it came in conflict with the Dharmasastras. The moderate school of Arthasastra-writers wanted nothing more than home-rule and were content to accept a fourfold classification of sciences. The later Dharmasastra-writers were clever men and often incorporated wholesale portions of Arthasastra material, but their point of view of politics remained different. Nemesis soon overtook the canonical writers on rajadharma ; and writers like Brihaspati and Usanas appeared on the scene, who relegated the sastras on dharma to the lumber-room and proclaimed the supremacy of the sastras having artha for their objective.

The Hindu doctrine of *trivarga*, the three categories of human life, is very old and is to be found in the Mahabharat(*a*). In the infancy of human civilisation all the vidyas are jumbled up together; and with the gradual development of culture, differentiation takes place(*b*). This is the case with the composition of *Dandaniti* by Brahma in the Mahabharat. A perusal of sec. 59 of the Santiparva will make it clear how comprehensive was the scope of Dandaniti. All the trivargas, nay, the chaturvargas, were described in it; and no other category of human life remains, when it is said that *Dharma* (virtue), *Artha* (wealth), *Kama* (pleasure) and *Moksa* (salvation) have been treated. Later on, separate sastras appeared for each of the trivargas. Thus in the Santiparva(*c*), Svayambhuba Manu is made to promulgate to the world the code of *Dharma*, while Brihaspati and Usanas also base their treatises on this comprehensive vidya. Brihaspati, so Vatsyayana(*d*) says, separated the *Artha* portions and thus became the founder of the science of Arthasastra, while Kamasastra was given shape by Nandin.

From our standpoint, the first two categories of human life, viz., dharma and artha are important,

(*a*) Later on another *varga, moksa*, was added. See *Santiparva*, sec. 59, 29-30, 72, 76.

(*b*) Synthetic philosophy is, no doubt, a product of later culture.

(*c*) Sec. 335 (Quoted, *Carmichael Lectures* 1918).

(*d*) *Kama-sutra* I, 7; II, 8-9 (Quoted, Barua, *Pre-Buddhistic Indian Philosophy*, p. 342).

because political literature worth the name is to be found in the sastras on dharma and sastras on artha. In the Dharmasutras and the Dharmasastras, politics is treated under the caption, Rajadharma or duties of the king. This kingly duty is the foundation of all other duties, and the concept of social order is the resultant of *swa-dharma* on the part of the king and the other classes in the society. No distinction is made, in the Rajadharma sections, between the personal and the public functions of the king, and none is necessary, in view of the fact that the fulfilment of all these functions is an indispensable preliminary to his own moral uplift ; and the concept of duty being very prominent in these sastras, the utilitarian character of statecraft is lost in ethical grandeur. The conception of canonical politics thus involves something more than the public functions of the king, and herein lies the clue in the evolution of Arthasastra politics. Politics, in the sacred sastras, has, for its pivot, the moral uplift of the king through the performance of his dharma, and the dharma of the king is the corner-stone of the dharma of the other classes. In other words, politics is a branch of social ethics, and the scope of politics has been widened by including political morality and moral rules *per se.*

Nevertheless, even in the earlier Dharmasutras, topics on artha were treated in the Rajadharma section ; and this is inevitable, since it is the dharma of the king to promote dharma, artha and kama among his subjects. It is not known, when, sastras on artha acquired an independent status, but the later Dharmasastras assume the existence of a separate sastra on artha. When therefore it is said that according to Caranavyuha of Saunaka, Arthasastra is an Upaveda of Atharvaveda(*a*), it may mean either of two things. Firstly it may mean that Arthasastra had not as yet acquired any autonomy and was still under the sway of sastras on dharma, or it may indicate the undue anxiety of the Brahmins to bring all sastras, secular though they might be, under the domain of the all-devouring Vedas. The second argument receives added weight when Kautilya(*b*) makes Arthasastra a branch of *Itihasa*, the latter in its turn being included within Trayi. D. R. Bhandarkar is of opinion that "at the outset of each Arthasastra were specified the occasion which led to its exposition and the sage by whom and the person or persons for whose edification it was discoursed. This explains why Kautilya places Arthasastra, like Purana and Dharmasastra, under Itihasa(*c*)."

However that might be, in course of time, Arthasastra came to its own. Kautilya's Arthasastra is the most important and comprehensive sastra on artha that has been handed down to us. There were writers on Arthasastra before Kautilya and their views are often mentioned by Kautilya only to be controverted by his own. Brihaspati is given credit by Vatsyayana as being the founder of the science of Arthasastra. In the Santiparva, Brihaspati is credited with an abridged edition of the original Dandaniti. Kautilya re-

(*a*) *Annals of the Bhandarkar Institute*, Vol. 7, pt. I, II p. 86.

(*b*) I, 3, 5 ; see later on.

(*c*) *Carmichael Lectures* 1918, pp. 107-8.

cords the fact that according to the Barhaspatyas there are only two sciences, Vartta and Dandaniti. Now how are we to reconcile all these apparently dissimilar things ?

The Dandaniti composed by Brahma is an encyclopædic vidya, dealing with the trivargas, dharma, artha and kama. Sec. 59 of the Santiparva read with sec. 335 enables us to conclude that the dharma portions of this encyclopædic Dandaniti were promulgated by Manu. In sec. 59 Brihaspati is said to have prepared an abridged edition and in sec. 335 Brihaspati is made to compose his treatise on the basis of the Dandaniti. Probably it was not so much an abridged edition of three thousand chapters, as the separation of the chapters dealing with the category of artha. Brihaspati was simply following in the wake of Manu. This assumption is justified in view of Vatsyayana's assertion. Again, Kautilya's assertion to the effect that the Barhaspatyas recognise only the sciences of Vartta and Dandaniti goes to strengthen our contention; because Vartta and Dandaniti deal with the artha category of human life, or, in other words, they deal with secular welfare. Vartta, which deals with agriculture, cattle-breeding and trade, has, no doubt, for its subject-matter, the acquisition of wealth or artha in its narrower sense. But Dandaniti, though different from Vartta, is a sastra on artha or secular welfare (broader sense) ; and hence Vatsyayana's assertion is nothing but the same as Kautilya's. We would further like to quote from Kamandaka. "According to the Barhaspatyas artha is man's objective and Vartta and Dandaniti are the only two sciences which help in the acquisition of artha(*a*)."

Kautilya's treatise is known by the name of Arthasastra. Now, what is the scope of Arthasastra and Dandaniti and also of Nitisastra. Hindu political thought is sometimes designated as raja-dharma(*b*) (duties of the king), sometimes as raja-sastra(*c*) (science of the king) or raja-vidya(*d*) and again as raja-niti(*e*) (rules of statecraft). It is again more or less equivalent to Dandaniti, Arthasastra and Nitisastra.

The scope can be determined by topical analysis and also by the definitions. Let us begin with Dandaniti. No technical book on Dandaniti is available, though in the fourfold classification of sciences Dandaniti occupies an honourable place. The topical analysis of Dandaniti is given in the Santiparva, but it is obvious. that there Dandaniti has gone beyond its limit; otherwise, why should moksa appear in it? The section, where the evolution of Dandaniti is described, is significant; it is the section dealing with matsyanyaya (anarchy) and the evolution of kingship. The objective of the author is to boom the science of Dandaniti and also to emphasize the fact so clearly stated by Kautilya that all other sciences and the progress of the world depend

(*a*) Kamandaka, *Nitisara* (Ganapati Sarkar), II, 4. Compare Sukra's definition of Arthasastra, IV-III, 110-11.

(*b*) *The raja-dharmanusasana-parva* of the Mahabharat; sections of the dharmasastras.

(*c*) *Santiparva.*

(*d*) *Kamandaka.*

(*e*) *Raja-niti-Ratnakar* by Chandeswara, published in *Journal B. O. R. Society.*

on Dandaniti. Dandaniti is then the fundamental science, but in the Santiparva, it has been made very comprehensive also. The error here involved is that a fundamental science should also be a comprehensive one, just as the modern science of sociology, the fundamental social science, was once thought to include all the specialized social sciences. It is curious that though Dandaniti has been taken for granted as an important vidya, neither Kautilya, nor Kamandaka, nor Sukra has cared to designate their treatises as treatises on Dandaniti. Literally Dandaniti means, niti or rules of danda. Now danda may mean punishment(*a*), or government(*b*). A third meaning may be given. The king is also called danda, because it is in the king that danda inheres(*c*). Therefore, the niti that guides the danda or king is Dandaniti or rajaniti. There is also a fourth meaning which is rather materialistic and which conclusively shows the *artha* character of Dandaniti. Kautilya says that Dandaniti is a means to make acquisitions, to keep them secure, to improve them and to distribute among the deserved the profits of improvement(*d*). The artha character of Dandaniti is self-evident in sec. 59 of the Santiparva, because there it is a *trivarga vidya*. But in sec. 140 artha-vidya has been equated with Dandaniti. "Repairing to Bharadwaja, he (Catrunjaya) asked the rishi about the truths of the science of Profit, saying,—How can an

(*a*) *Arthasastra*, I,4.

(*b*) *Nayanayau* and *Balabale*. *Ibid*, I,2.

(*c*) See *Kamandakaniti*, II, 15 and *Sukraniti* I, 313-14.

(*d*) I,4. See later on. Brihaspati's characterisation of vartta and dandaniti as artha-vidya will now be clear.

unacquired object be acquired? How again when acquired, can it be increased? How also, when increased, can it be protected? And how when protected, should it be used?" And the answer of the rishi is a significant discourse on statecraft. Kamandaka(*a*) and Sukra(*b*) accept Dandaniti in its political sense. But Kamandaka has given an artha bias when he describes the fourfold functions of the king as acquisition of wealth, its protection, increase and well-deserved distribution(*c*). Thus we see the artha character of Dandaniti. Sometimes it is equated with sastras on artha; sometimes it is the parent of sastras on artha, while more commonly it is a branch of artha-sastra or rather sastra on artha.

We have interpreted Dandaniti from four standpoints, viz., rules of punishment or restraint, rules of government, rules (private and public) for the king and the materialistic rules. The first three meanings are more or less identical and can be classed together, while the last one should be kept distinct.

Dandaniti has been translated by Jayaswal(*d*) as 'Ethics of the Executive'. The translation is not accurate. Firstly, it does not indicate the materialistic bias of the science. Then again, the rendering is apt for raja-dharma, where there is an ethical bias; but in Dandaniti there is no predominance of ethics: it is a distinct species of political morality, unconditioned by rules of common morality. The rendering

(*a*) II, 15. (*b*) I, 313-14.

(*c*) I, 18 (Ganapati Sarkar). Manu has given a similar catalogue.

(*d*) *Calcutta Weekly Notes*, Vol. 15, p. cclxxv.

of danda by the word 'Executive' is accurate and the general rendering of the term (if we exclude the fourth meaning) might be "Statecraft."

The school of Brihaspati recognise the validity of the artha sciences, viz., Vartta and Dandaniti, while the school of Usanas declare that Dandaniti is *the* science. The fundamental and probably the comprehensive character of the science impressed Usanas(*a*).

Kautilya, unlike Brihaspati and Usanas, accepts the fourfold classification of sciences, but his treatise is known as Arthasastra. His Arthasastra describes the requisites of a good king, the ministry, the spy system, the economic and industrial functions of the state, the civil and criminal law, the foreign policy and the art of warfare. His sastra is a treatise on politics, no doubt, and thus comes under the sastras of artha category ; but his politics, and this is significant, is intensely dominated by materialism and principles of vartta, the subject matter of which is artha in a narrower sense. In other words, his Arthasastra is Dandaniti (in the narrower sense) and principles of vartta from the standpoint of the king. In the traditional fourfold classification Dandaniti is merely political(*b*) ; but Kautilya, who was throughout dominated by the policy of expansion and acquisition wanted to give his science a materialistic turn. This is the reason why he in the fourth chapter of the first book, defines Dandaniti in a way which will suit his own purpose. But probably he thought that this would only

(*a*) Compare Aristotle's conception of politics.

(*b*) *Arthasastra,* I, 2.

confuse the scope of Dandaniti(*a*), and hence he named his sastra as Arthasastra. In the last book, Kautilya has given us his definition of Arthasastra and this will help us in having an idea as to its scope.

The interpretation put by Jayaswal(*b*) on this passage is not tenable. He interprets *artha* as society and says that the first category can be realised in the family, the second, artha, in the society and the third can be realised by oneself alone. This evidently carries no meaning and we may dismiss his translation which is based on these untenable assumptions. It would not be going too far, if we say, that the significance of the definition has not yet been fully appreciated. When Kautilya in the last book says that *artha* is the *vritti* of man, he is evidently thinking of the science of *vartta*; and again when he says that a territory containing human beings is termed *artha*, he is evidently thinking of the central figure (the king) of his sastra to whom his *rajya* is related as wealth to a man. The acquisition and protection and expansion of such a territory with the help of the principles of *vartta* form the subject-matter of Arthasastra. In other words, Kautilyan Arthasastra is Dandaniti regulated for the purpose of acquisition of *public artha*. Hence Arthasastra is a sastra on artha in a two-fold sense. It deals with Dandaniti and therefore it is a secular or artha-vidya. Again, its purpose is the acquisition of wealth, territory

(*a*) But in the Mahabharat there was such confusion.

(*b*) *Calcutta Weekly Notes*, Vol. 15, p.cclxxv. See also *Hindu Polity*, part I, p.5.

(artha) ; therefore it is an Arthasastra. But this is public acquisition or public vartta. This aspect is evident, if we turn our attention to Book II, p. 262 and 305 and the opening lines of the book.

If in p. 9 of the Arthasastra, Dandaniti is taken to mean an Artha-science in the narrower sense(*a*), then the scope of the two sciences Dandaniti and Arthasastra is similar ; but if we interpret the relevant passage to mean that Dandaniti is the *upaya* or means by adopting which the king can increase artha (public) or territory, then of course the scope of Dandaniti is narrower than that of Arthasastra. Arthasastra will then mean the art of Government with a view to public acquisition(*b*).

Kautilyan Arthasastra, though not one of the traditional sciences, is nevertheless a sastra on artha, both in the narrow and broad senses. But then it is curious that Kautilya should enter it under the head Itihasa(*c*), the latter again being entered under the Vedas(*d*). The explanation is three-fold. Firstly, "Kautilya seeks to bring the science into line with the principles of the sacred canon(*e*)." The second explanation lies in the manner of its exposition(*f*). The third explanation seeks to show that the principles of polity are often derived from Itihasa and hence

(*a*) In the narrower sense artha is the subject-matter of vartta only ; in the broader sense artha is taken to mean secular welfare, the second category of human life.

(*b*) Sukra views Arthasastra as both Dandaniti and acquisition of wealth. Probably it refers to acquisition by the king, though that is not mentioned in the sloka.

(*c*) I, 5. (*d*) I, 3.

(*e*) *Sir Ashutosh Jubilee Volumes, Orientalia* I, p. 58.

(*f*) *Carmichael Lectures* 1918, pp. 107-8.

Itihasa or history might be said to be the root of which the fruit is politics. This is not our conjecture, but Kautilya himself conceives of a case where "the ministers, through the medium of the king's favourites, teach him the principles of polity with illustrations taken from the Itihasa and Purana(*a*)." Of course it is to be admitted that the last two explanations do not explain the second part of the proposition.

Latterly however, the technical terms Dandaniti and Arthasastra were superseded by the term Nitisastra. Kamandaka in his Nitisastra follows in the footsteps of Kautilya; but an analysis of the topics, dealt with in his book, will reveal the fact that Kamandaka has given a wide berth to the "law" portions of the Arthasastra and has scrupulously kept himself aloof from the economic or vartta portions of Kautilya's book. Kamandaka accepts the traditional fourfold classification of sciences and emphasises the predominance of Dandaniti over other sciences(*b*). But this Dandaniti, which is but another name for Rajaniti because raja is called danda, is regulated by certain other rules and hence it is called Nitisastra. In spite of the economic(*c*) nature of the duties of the king, Kamandaka's treatise is eminently political and does not treat economic *niti* or social niti from the standpoint of private individuals(*d*). It is called Nitisastra, because there must be some sort

(*a*) V, 6. For examples, see I, 6. Compare Sukra's definition of Itihasa, IV-II, 102-3.

(*b*) II, 9.

(*c*) I, 18.

(*d*) Negligible exceptions.

of restraint or regulation behind kingly functions and hence the importance of *vinaya* or discipline in the king's curriculum. Kamandaka's treatise undisguisedly treats of political niti from the standpoint of the king; so much so, that he designates it as raja-vidya or interprets Dandaniti to mean in effect raja-niti. But it must not be understood that his political niti is in any way conditioned by general rules of morality, for when public good requires it, the king must not hesitate to set at nought the ordinary rules of dharma(*a*).

Sukra's work though known as Nitisara is more comprehensive than that of Kamandaka, and in a sense, the scope is much wider than that of Kautilyan Arthasastra, though the economic aspect does not receive so much emphasis(*b*). Sukraniti treats of kingship, state officials, offences and punishment, administration of justice, foreign policy and warfare, economic tit-bits, social customs and general rules of morality. Apart from this topical analysis which clearly shows its encyclopaedic character, the author himself at the beginning of his book defines the scope of his work. The science is the most fundamental social science and is the "spring of virtue, wealth, enjoyment and salvation"; and at the same time it is most practical or rather utilitarian, for "without niti the stability of no man's affairs can be maintained". But though it is useful to all, yet "the whole duty of man, nay the entire human personality, acquires a significance, only in so far as it is conditioned or moti-

(*a*) VI, 5-13; XIX, 71.

(*b*) It is not neglected. See II and IV-II; V, 77-9; III 362-9.

vated by danda(*a*)." Thus the political niti predominates in Sukraniti and it is obvious, because Sukra makes the king the creator of epochs. Nitisastra, in so far it is political, is rather an art and political speculations couched in imperative mood look like art, though that is not always true(*b*).

Sukraniti mentions the sciences of Dandaniti and Arthasastra, but his book is known as a sastra on *niti*. His sastra is essentially a sastra on artha in the broader sense. though he does not seem to be so materialistic in his outlook as Kautilya. He defines Dandaniti in its political sense and so defines Arthasastra as not to give any undue emphasis on its economic aspect, though he includes economics under it. He seems to follow a *via media* between the rajadharma school of Manu and others and the Arthasastra schools of Kautilya and his followers. (Compare III, 2-5 and V, 77-9) His book breathes of secularism, but he tries to make it a synthetic art of life and says that the chaturvargas have their root in it(*c*). The fact that he is trying to steer a middle course is evident, when he tries to make politics sometimes conditioned by and sometimes independent of the rules of ordinary morality(*d*). Sukra is never an advocate of rigid and hidebound rules of morality, he is essentially a man of this matter-of-fact world: but he is convinced that happiness, which

(*a*) Sarkar, *Pos. Back. of Hindu Sociology*, Book II, pt. I, p. 29.

(*b*) See my article, "*The Arthasastra of K. and the Nitisastra of S.*"

(*c*) I, 10-11 ; III, 2-5.

(*d*) See my article, "*The Arthasastra of* etc."

is the end of mankind, can not be attained without dharma or morality(*a*). Hence the utility of discipline, restraint and political organisation ; and herein lies the difference in the point of view between the Kamasastra-writers and Nitisastra-writers.

The rajadharma-writers treated politics as a branch of ethics, but the Arthasastra-writers completely separated the two. "As Bodin corrected the Machiavellian conception of a total severance and takes the middle ground," so our Sukra assumes dharma or moral law controlling political facts from a higher plane ; and thus he works out a comprehensive, synthetic and harmonized art of social life. Nevertheless, Sukra himself is often perplexed as to what should be the proper relation between political niti and dharma or ethics(*b*). Probably this confusion emboldened Magha to define niti as having only two aims : one's own rising and conquering the enemy(*c*).

Hindu political thought of the Arthasastra and the Nitisastra type is pre-eminently political and therefore more detailed than the politics of the sacred canon ; but Manu had such an unlimited credit that his canonical politics is hardly to be distinguished from secular politics in point of *material*. But the theoretical background remains distinct.

Hindu political thought is saturated with intense realism, and with some exceptions (*d*), it is not at all

(*a*) III, 2-3.
(*b*) See Ch. V.
(*c*) Quoted by Winternitz, *Calcutta Review* April, 1924, p.3.
(*d*) Portions of Santiparva ; Buddhist theory of kingship etc.

speculative, *i.e.*, it does not deal with the theory and philosophy of state. It deals with the concrete problems of state as it is: hence the treatises seem to be treatises on the art of government and acquisition. Nevertheless, the writers are often dominated by political ideals, *e.g.* ideals of universal sovereignty. But even the problems of government are treated from the standpoint of the king, and the concept of 'peoples and their rights' seems never to have made any bold impression upon the minds of writers, both secular and canonical. Probably this is the greatest defect of Hindu political writers(*a*). In a sense, this is the original sin inherited by the secular school from the writers on raja-dharma, who treated politics as a species of duty enjoined on the *king*. From this standpoint, rajadharma is on an equal footing with the varnasram dharma. While secular writers disentangled the political science from the thraldom of sacred canon and separated, at least in theory, the public from the private functions of the king, they forgot that the king who was the centre of raja-dharma politics, need not be so in the secular one. Of course there is some justification when we view some of the books as manuals prepared for the guidance of princes. But it is to be wondered at that the Hindus, who were so famous as abstruse philosophers, should be so matter-of-fact in their treatment of politics.

A word might be said about the method employed in Hindu political treatises. Historical method in its

(*a*) Let us hope future researches will be able to controvert this statement.

extreme form cannot be suitable to social vidyas ; but deductive method and empiricism (psychological facts etc.), supplemented by historical method, seem to be the proper course. This is the method adopted by the Hindus, and Kautilya, Sukra and Kamandaka have utilized the Pauranic and historical examples, not infrequently(*a*). Of course, there is no use denying the fact that the method is historical in appearance.

(*a*) *Kamandaka*, I, 14, 54, 56-8 ; VII, 51-4 ; IX, 11, 51, 53, 61, 66 ; XI, 7, 7(*1*), 8, 10, 17, 21, 22, 31 ; XII, 7 ; XV, 50-55, 63-4; XVII,57; XVIII, 20-3, 41, 44, 56, 58-9 ; XIX, 71. *Sukraniti*, I, 111-5, 135-8, 217-8, 225-6, 283-4, 287-92; II, 20-1, 78-9, 81-5 ; IV-II, 24 ; IV-IV, 80-1 ; IV-VII, 494-5, 726-7; V, 36, 118-9. *Kautilya*, I, 6, 20 etc.

THE HINDU VIEW OF THE STATE OF NATURE

In the Santiparva of the Mahabharat we come across several remarkable pictures of the ante-political conditions of man and it will be our endeavour to present them as vividly as possible and also to analyse that state into its constituent elements and to bring out the significance of the same. It should be pointed out that the treatment (*a*) in the Santiparva is not part of a systematic political treatise and hence we would not be justified in looking for Hobbesian reasoning and system in a work like that; but the treatment as a whole is rich enough to warrant us in drawing certain conclusions: an adequate knowledge of which is essential for a right comprehension of the Hindu conception of the state.

With section 15 we begin. Yudhisthira was so much sorrow-stricken for the loss of his kinsmen in battle that he even thought of renouncing his kingdom and sovereignty. All the four brothers, nay, Kunti and Draupadi, sought to dissuade him from leading the life of a recluse; but it is with the speech of Arjuna, covering the whole of the fifteenth section, that we are concerned. Arjuna delivers a brilliant

(*a*) We take three instances, (*i*) sec. 15, (*ii*) sec. 59, (*iii*) secs. 67 and 68.

panegyric on the nature and functions of *danda*(*a*) and seeks to impress upon Yudhisthira the fact that without danda 'creatures would soon be destroyed,' and 'like fish in the water, stronger animals (would) prey on the weaker.' 'If there were no danda in the world distinguishing the good from the bad, then the whole world would have been enveloped in utter darkness and all things would have been confounded. Even they that are breakers of rules, that are atheists and scoffers of the Vedas, afflicted by chastisement (danda), soon become disposed to observe rules and restrictions.' 'If chastisement could not inspire fear, then ravens and beasts of prey would have eaten up all other animals and men and the clarified butter intended for sacrifices.' 'If chastisement did not uphold and protect, then ravage and confusion would have set in on every side, and all barriers would have been swept away and the idea of property would have disappeared.' 'If the rod of chastisement be not uplifted, the dog will lick the sacrificial butter. The crow also would take away the first sacrificial offering, if that rod were not kept uplifted.' 'If chastisement did not uphold and protect, then nobody would have studied the Vedas, nobody would have milked a milch cow, and no maiden would have married (*b*).'

(*a*) *Danda* may mean punishment, the royal sceptre or the army. Often it stands for *executive power in the abstract* of which the concrete symbol is the royal sceptre. Here it is used in the abstract sense. See *Santiparva*, sec. 121 where danda is described as an awe-inspiring person. Compare *Manu*, VII, 14 ; 17 ; 27. See Kamandaka, *Nitisara*, II, 36-43 ; *Sukraniti*, I, 313-14 ; *Arthasastra*, I,4 ; *Gautama*, XI, 28.

(*b*) *Santiparva* (tr. P. C. Roy), sec. 15.

All the above quotations are taken from the fifteenth section and illustrate in a vivid way the state of man when the restraining influence of danda is absent. It is the danda of the king which transforms the non-state into the state (*a*).

From the above quotations, it will be evident that three things are not possible in the state of *matsyanyaya* *i.e.* anarchy. (1) Religion and morality cannot be practised, *e. g.* the ravens would have eaten up the clarified butter and nobody would have studied the Vedas. (2) 'The idea of property would have disappeared.' (3) In the absence of danda there cannot be any family life, because the maidens would practise free love and would not marry.

In other words, the *trivargas* of life, *dharma*, *artha* and *kama* are all dependent on danda and hence cannot be even conceived in the non-state. The attributes, then, which differentiate the state from matsyanyaya, are the trivargas made possible by the danda of the king (*b*).

The picture of this pre-political state is therefore a picture of warfare in which the stronger animals prey on the weaker. So far it is Hobbeslike. Again, it is the danda of the king which distinguishes the good from the bad (*c*). In other words, there is no standard

(*a*) In this connection, see sec. 167 where Bhisma narrates the creation of the universe, the wicked doings of the *Danavas*, and finally, the creation of a *sword* by Brahman with the help of which Rudra established order. The section is highly suggestive.

(*b*) Sec. 15, sl. 2, 3.

(*c*) Sl. 32.

of conduct, and unless there is some rule, we cannot judge conduct, and a rule is worthless, unless it is backed up by danda. Hobbes also says that in the state of nature there exists no distinction of right and wrong. The idea of property is absent in non-state(*a*) and Hobbes says, 'that is every man's that he can get, and for so long as he can keep it(*b*).' There can be no knowledge (*c*), no corn or wealth (*d*) in such a state, just as in the Hobbesian state of nature there can be no 'industry' or 'culture of the earth', 'no arts' and 'no letters'. The pre-political state is not a social state ; it is a state of 'ravage and confusion', 'destruction' and 'darkness of hell'. In Hobbes' description of human psychology the social instincts are entirely ignored.

Hobbes' delineation of the state of nature does not suggest that such a state had a general historical existence, though he says, that every man, when taking a journey, arms himself ; when going to sleep, locks his doors and does such other things ; thereby showing his distrust for fellow-beings. So Arjuna's speech does not suggest that his state of nature—a state in which chaos reigns supreme—had a real historical existence on the face of this earth. On the other hand, his conception of *matsyanyaya* is a thing of speculation, logically deduced from a study of the essential nature of the concept *danda*—the central theme of this section. The concept danda is the most important and an ever-recurring concept in the Hindu literature on politics

(*a*) Sl. 30. (*b*) *Leviathan,* Ch. 13. (*c*) Sl. 40.
(*d*) Sl. 4.

and its presence makes a state, while its absence creates a matsyanyaya. Arjuna's description of the state of nature is logically related to his description of the nature of danda: the historical aspect recedes entirely into the background and the philosophical aspect comes to the fore. Hobbes also disregards the historical aspect, an aspect which received some sympathetic literary treatment at the hands of the 15th century European Aeneas Sylvius(*a*)—but from a different standpoint. His state of nature is neither historical, nor correlated to the nature of danda, but is a logical deduction from his psychological assumptions(*b*), however incomplete they may be.

We next take up section 59. Yudhisthira put to Bhisma a very significant question. "Possessed of hands and arms and neck like others, having an understanding and senses like those of others, subject like others to the same kinds of joy and grief, endued with back, mouth and stomach similar to those of the rest of the world, having vital fluids and bones and marrow and flesh and blood similar to those of the rest of the world, inhaling and exhaling breaths like others, possessed of life-breaths and bodies like other men, resembling others in birth and death, in fact similar to others in respect of all the attributes of humanity, for what reason does one man, *viz.*, the king, govern the rest of the world numbering many men possessed of great intelligence and bravery(*c*)." The question is,

(*a*) Dunning, *Political Theories, Ancient and Mediaeval*, pp. 282-3.

(*b*) *Ibid*, *From Luther to Montesquieu*, p. 268.

(*c*) Sl. 6-8.

in effect, a question about the justification of the king's authority.

Bhisma's answer to this question gives us a picture of the pre-political state and the way in which the state emerged and the justification of the royal authority.

At first (mark the historical and the realistic touch) there was no political society(*a*), no king, no danda and no dandika (wielder of danda). All men used to protect one another righteously(*b*). "As they thus lived, O Bharata, righteously protecting one another, they found the task (after sometime) to be painful. Error then began to assail their hearts. Having become subject to error, the perceptions of men, O prince, came to be clouded and thence their virtue began to decline. When their perceptions were dimmed and when men became subject to error, all of them became covetous, O chief of the Bharatas. And because men sought to obtain objects which they did not possess, another passion called lust (of acquisition) got hold of them. When they became subject to lust, another passion named wrath soon soiled them. Once subject to wrath, they lost all consideration of what should be done and what not. Unrestrained sexual indulgence set in. Men began to utter what they chose. All distinctions between food that is clean and unclean and between

(*a*) Here the Sanskrit word *rajyam* should be translated as 'political society' and not as 'sovereignty' as P.C. Roy (Sl. 13-4) and U. Ghoshal (*Hindu Political Theories*, p. 176) have done. It is also better than monarchy. (Jayaswal, *Hindu Polity*, I, pp. 97-8).

(*b*) With the help of *dharma*—'*dharmenaiba*'.

virtue and vice disappeared. When this confusion set in amongst men, the Vedas disappeared. Upon the disappearance of the Vedas, righteousness was lost(*a*)." We are not concerned here with the remaining portions of this section which describe how the gods (mark, it is not the people), stricken with fear, went to Brahma and sought for a remedy. The result was the composition of *Dandaniti*(*b*).

The description of the state of nature in the above extract is given as an incident in the creation of kingship and the picture is so drawn as to suggest that the state of nature had an objective reality. There are two stages in this state of nature : one is a social state in which the people protect one another righteously. The restraining influence of danda is not thought necessary, a feeling of justice (dharma) governs men's conduct. So far it resembles the state of nature of Pufendorf and Locke. We might go further and equate the dharma governing men's conduct with the law of nature and the dictates of right reason postulated by Pufendorf and Locke. But the second stage in the state of nature is a period of growing degeneration, and sooner or later a regular pandemonium sets in, from which mankind is saved by the intervention of the gods.

Jayaswal takes the first stage in the above state of nature to be a 'non-ruler state,' an 'extreme democracy(*c*).' Probably it was not a political society,

(*a*) *Santiparva*, sec. 59, sl. 15-21.
(*b*) After that the gods went to Vishnu for a king. The subsequent passages describe the installation of Prithu by gods and sages.
(*c*) *Hindu Polity*, Part I, pp. 97-9 and footnotes.

because danda was conspicuous by its absence. At best it would resemble a society pictured by the philosophical anarchists(*a*).

The transition, from the first stage in the state of nature to the second stage, is not explained anymore beyond saying that men began to commit errors, owing to their perception having become clouded (*moha*). So, in Rousseau, a growing degeneracy is postulated, though it is not clear whether Rousseau viewed the state of nature as a historical reality or an ideal condition, because he 'continually oscillates between the actual and the ideal(*b*).' The second stage is fatal to the enjoyment of the *trivargas*; for there can be no *artha*(*c*) when every one is covetous; there can be no *kama* when unrestrained sexual indulgence sets in; and finally there can be no *dharma* when all distinctions between virtue and vice disappear. We again come back to our old thesis that a condition of matsyanyaya is intolerable and that for the establishment of the trivargas danda must be enforced in accordance with the rules of dandaniti, and this is what is meant when Brahma announces the composition of the Dandaniti to the assembled gods(*d*).

In the above description, the birth of the state is due to a growing moral depravity on the part of

(*a*) For an impartial review of the ideals of the philosophical anarchists, see Jethro Brown, *The Underlying Principles of Modern Legislation*, Prologue.

(*b*) *Social Contract, Introduction* by Tozer, p. 38.

(*c*) In Locke's state of nature there is private property, *Civil Government*, II, ch. 5; see *Santiparva*, sec. 57, sl. 40.

(*d*) *Santiparva*, sec. 59, sl. 75-8. A fourth *varga* is often added, see sl. 79. See *Sukraniti*, III, 2-5.

mankind. The necessity of the danda and hence of the state is evident when we see that the recluse in the forest and even the mendicant take to their swadharma through fear of punishment(*a*). In the golden age, when mankind is highly moral, it is possible to dispense with the agency of the state, and this is hinted at in the beginning of Bhisma's discourse. Therefore human psychology and the birth of state are logically related.

We pass on to consider the third extract(*b*) from the Mahabharat bearing on the state of nature. Bhisma is explaining to Yudhisthira the importance on the part of a people of first selecting a king, because the king, the wielder of danda, is the stay of all. The manner in which Bhisma is speaking is reminiscent of narrating a mythological story. The state of nature as depicted in the two sections invariably reminds us of Hobbes and something more, if that is conceivable. In days of old, in consequence of anarchy, men met with destruction, devouring one another like stronger fishes devouring the weaker ones in the water(*c*). In such a state, the strong would forcibly appropriate the possession of the weak and if the latter refuse to surrender them with ease, their very lives will be taken. Nobody then, with reference to any article in his possession, would be able to say, this is mine(*d*). To make matters worse, the ill-got wealth of the strong would again be snatched by others and then they would sigh for a king(*e*).

(*a*) *Ibid*, sec. 15, sl. 12.

(*b*) *Santiparva*, sec. 67-8. (*c*) Sec. 67, sl. 17. (*d*) Sec. 68, sl. 14-5. (*e*) Sec. 67, sl. 13.

6

Even aged fathers and mothers would not escape molestation and injury at the hands of their children(*a*). All restrictions about marriage and intercourse would cease, marriage would not take place and the very existence of society will be at stake(*b*). The catalogue is fairly long, but the above extract will give us a fair idea of the state of matsyanyaya.

But the above state is intolerable and the people, in order to escape from the evils of anarchy, assemble and make certain compacts, saying,—"he who becomes harsh in speech, or violent in temper, he who seduces or abducts other people's wives, or robs the wealth that belong to others, should be cast off by us(*c*)." They lived for a time in this civil community which seems to be a republic. But sooner or later they were tired of this community and went to Brahma and asked him to select some one as their king(*d*). At first there is the Hobbesian state of nature, then a republican state, and finally the emergence of a monarchic state. In the above sketch, the pre-political condition is also a pre-social state.

In the first sketch, the concept of *matsyanyaya* is essentially a philosophic concept, logically correlated to the contradictory concept of *danda*. The second

(*a*) Sl. 18. (*b*) Sl. 21-2.

(*c*) Sec. 67, sl. 17-8. (*d*) Sl. 19-20. Ghoshal thinks that the civil community before the birth of the monarchic state is a society without a political superior (see p. 179), but this is not correct; because the state then formed was a republican state. The significance of the 20th sloka is that the republican form of government did not work.

sketch starts with a mythically perfect age, in which there is no danda or king, followed by a period of degeneration, which necessitated the birth of a political society. Here the historical aspect is predominant, but not necessarily submerging the rational point of view, since the state is the result of man's moral depravity. In the third sketch also the historical point of view is specially important.

The Hindu concept of the state of nature has been approached from three different standpoints. Let us take the first standpoint, *i.e. Primeval Chaos.* (1) Hindu theories of creation often postulate the existence of a primeval chaos, when there was neither aught nor nought. The eternal Being seized with a will to create brought order out of this chaos. So the king, who is of a divine nature(*a*), is thought to have brought order out of chaos by the exercise of his danda. Here Hindu political thought is indebted to Hindu metaphysics and in succeeding ages the whole thing assumed the character of having an objective reality. (2) The concept has again been approached from an empirical angle based on utilitarian ground. The object was to eulogise the benefits of a monarchic state. People actually saw the evils of anarchy, which made their appearance when the powerful danda of the king was withdrawn, and they were probably cognizant(*b*) of the failures of republican states. Probably, in this case, the birth of the concept was a matter of *experience.* (3) Lastly, the

(*a*) Vishnu entered Prithu's body. *Santiparva*, sec. 59 sl. 128.

(*b*) *Ibid*, sec. 67, sl. 17-20.

concept may be viewed as an offspring of pure speculative thought. The process of thinking was this. What is the fundamental attribute of a state and what are the objects of a state ? To the first question, the answer was danda, and to the second, the enjoyment of the trivargas or even chaturvargas (3 or 4 aims of life). Now, if these are the essential features of a state, surely, their absence,—so the process of reasoning runs—is a necessary corollary of a non-state. The process of reasoning is, at first, analytic and then the method of elimination is adopted. Here the concept is purely *logical*(*a*).

In the Buddhist literature(*b*), we also come across some pictures of the pre-political condition of mankind. The description is in the form of a historical narrative and merely traces the origin of kingship and explains why a king is called a Mahasammata and a Khattriya. Here, as in sec. 59 of the Santiparva, the state of nature may be divided into two stages, of which the first one seems to be an era of bliss. Because of inquisitiveness and desire for food the primitive beings took to eating the rime which formed on the surface of the ocean and earth mingled together. "The complexion of those who ate but little of this food was clear, whereas that of those who ate much of it was dark." In this way distinctions arose, and "they, whose complexion was

(*a*) In *Santiparva*, sec. 15 the concept seems to be purely logical.

(*b*) I follow Rockhill's *Life of the Buddha*, pp. 1-7. The story is also to be found in the Agganna—suttanta of the *Dighanikaya*.

clear, were proud of it and became sinful and iniquitous." Thus a period of gradual degeneration sets in and this is the second stage of the state of nature. The distinction of sexes became prominent because of eating rice and the inevitable result of this was the evolution of love, lust and fornication. The conception of wrong was gradually emerging, but a wrongdoer feels insulted, when someone exclaims, 'thou doest that which is wrong(*a*).' The institutions of family and property make their appearance as a result of *contract*(*b*), but it is soon found, that some people do not respect the sanctity of property rights in the pre-political society. When a man whose food has been stolen complains to others, saying, that he has been wronged, the thief is reprimanded; but the men, who laid hold of the thief and brought him before all, are also reprimanded because of their bringing him into their midst(*c*). Such a state of society is surely unbearable and the only way to escape lies in choosing one who will be the protector of the fields and who will receive the homage of all.

The above picture strongly suggests that the pre-political stages had some objective reality, but the institutions of family and property can only be logically thought of as parts of one whole. Historically they may appear before political society; but logically, *i. e.* in the order of thought, the concept of Mahasammata, 'the lord of the law' must come first. And this is what is meant in the following lines which are quoted

(*a*) Rockhill, *Life* etc. p. 4.

(*b*) *Ibid*, pp. 4-6; Cf. Locke, *Civil Govt.* II, 5.

(*c*) *Ibid*, p. 6.

from the same story. "Now, this is the first appearance in the world of a system of boundary lines, and this (boundary) is right or not right according to the king's decision, and he is the lord of the law(*a*)". This refers to the legalisation of property rights. Again, the following lines refer to the institution of family life. "And thus it was that what was formerly considered unlawful has become lawful now-a-days, etc(*b*)."

In such a state of nature, which is a social state(*c*), we can think of *artha* and *kama*—property and family life; but the enjoyment thereof is uncertain; for there is no common standard by which a particular conduct can be judged and no political superior who will punish the violation of rights. As in Locke, property-rights seem to exist in the state of nature, and the main reason—we might say, the sole reason—for the institution of kingship (Mahasammata) can be found in the etymology of the word 'Khattriya' which means, "Protector of the fields"(*d*). In other words, the justification of the state seems to lie in its enforcement of pre-existing property-rights—the word "property" being understood in its comprehensive sense.

(*a*) Rockhill, *Life* etc. p. 6.
(*b*) *Ibid*, p. 5.
(*c*) Bhandarkar (*Carmichael Lectures* 1918, p.122) is wrong when he says that "the state of nature is a state of war". He has overlooked the point that there are *two* stages in the state of nature as found in the Dighanikaya. The first stage is a period of bliss, while the second one is still a social state and not a state of war; none the less it has some disadvantages, which lead to the creation of a ruler. In sec. 59 of the Santiparva again, the first stage of the state of nature is not a state of war; it is a state when people protect one another righteously.
(*d*) The Mahasammata is also called Khattriya. See p.7, *Life of the Buddha*.

We have finished the typical descriptions of the state of nature. Sometimes, it is a state of bliss, sometimes, a state of uncertainty, while more often it is a state of war. The Buddhistic conception of the state of nature did not make its influence felt in subsequent writings; but the conception of the state of nature as a state of anarchy, in which, people devour one another (as stronger fishes swallow the weaker ones), was so attractive and handy as to have given birth to a technical word, *viz.*, matsyanyaya. The idea occurs in the Ramayana(*a*), where it is said that in a kingless country, nobody is one's own, and there the people eat up one another as fishes do. Kautilya uses the term at least twice(*b*) and from two different standpoints. In the first instance, he takes his stand on *rational* ground and explains the fundamental importance of the concept danda and also points out the relation between *matsyanyaya* and *danda*. In the second instance, he uses the word in connection with the election of Vaivasvata Manu, the first king, and thus hints at its *historic* reality. Manu also assumes an antecedent state of nature which is a state of confusion and chaos(*c*). Kamandaka(*d*) again uses the technical term matsyanyaya and this occurs where he is eulogising danda, much in the same manner as Kautilya in the first instance. In Kamandaka the method of approach is rather from the logical standpoint. The concept again appears in a Purana(*e*) in connection

(*a*) II, 67, 31.
(*b*) *Arthasastra*, I, 4; I, 13.
(*c*) *Manu*, VII, 20-21.
(*d*) *Nitisara*, II, 40.
(*e*) *Matsya Purana* (S. B. H. Vol. 17 part 2, p. 238).

with a description of the nature of danda, and finally, to crown all, mention is made of matsyanyaya in the Khalimpur copper-plate charter of Dharmapala of Pala dynasty(*a*). From all this, it will be evident, how thoroughly ingrained was this idea in the Hindu mind and how matsyanyaya became a by-word in Hindu political literature, both secular and canonical.

(*a*) The inscription is quoted in *Banglar Itihasa* Vol. I, 2nd edition p. 171 footnote. by Rakhaldas Banerjee. See also pp. 171-3.

ORIGIN OF KINGSHIP

THE concept of *danda* is one of the most fundamental concepts in the Hindu political theory, and therefore, it is but natural, that the king, the wielder of this danda, would occupy much space in the writings of the philosophers of the Arthasastra and the Nitisastra school and a not inconsiderable one in those of the Dharmasastra school. The present state of knowledge warrants us in concluding that political theory exclusively concerned itself with monarchic state, and we are not disposed to accept the view advanced by R. C. Majumdar(a) that 'a new epoch of political thought' was ushered in by the speculations, in the Santiparva, merely because there are one or two sections(b) in the former, dealing with the problem of the *ganas*. These sections might be the result of the politics of the post-Kautilyan ganas,—an instance of political thought being profoundly influenced by political environment,—but it would be going too far, if we say, that a new epoch is

(a) *Corporate Life in Ancient India*, pp. 257-68, 2nd edition. On *arajaka* constitution see *Hindu Polity*, I, pp. 171-4 and for an opposite view, see *Indian Historical Quarterly* Vol. I, No. 2, p. 380 and pp. 395-6.

(b) *Santiparva*, sec. CVII and sec. LXXXI, the latter dealing with the affairs of the Andhaka-Vrishni league.

introduced, when we know, that in the succeeding ages, this line of thought was not at all developed.

The problem of the origin of kingship might be viewed from two standpoints, (1) Realistic and (2) Rationalistic. From the former standpoint, the problem resolves itself into the manner in which kingship actually did originate; while the latter standpoint concerns itself mainly with the question of the justification of the institution of kingship, The one is mainly concerned with historical explanation, the other with the question of moral justification. Analytically, the two problems are different, but often it seems exceedingly difficult to extricate the one from the other.

In the Vedic ages there is no political literature worth the name and there are only scattered references from which we can know something about the origin and institution of kingship. It is a matter of common knowledge that consolidation and growth of royal power in the early ages is mainly the result of external pressure. Democracy is even now-a-days(*a*) ill-suited to the exigencies of external pressure like warfare, and, as in the case of the primitive Teutons, the Indo-Aryans also had to take recourse to the institution of kingship in their continuous warfare against the Asuras, the non-Aryans. It is the realistic standpoint that is implied in a passage in the Aitareya Brahman(*b*), where the Devas, realising that they were being

(*a*) Compare the evolution of war-cabinet in England during the Great War and the dictatorial powers assumed by the American President in times of warfare. (Lincoln's dictatorship in the American Civil War)

(*b*) Jayaswal, *Hindu Polity*, II, pp. 4-5.

defeated by the Asuras, because they had no kings, proceeded to elect one as king. The utilitarian aspect is also patent. The Vedic kingship is a human institution, and it cannot be otherwise, when kings are selected and can be deposed. In the later Vedas, some sort of divinity is often ascribed to the king, but then it is in connection with the sacrifices performed by the king, and this identification is only temporary(*a*). But the ascription of this divinity is not at all significant, because the whole Khattriya class, of which the king is a member, is also of divine origin ;—nay, the Brahmins are of divine origin. In the Satapatha-Brahman however, the problem of the origin of kingship seems to be viewed from the rationalistic standpoint. The right to rule is sought to be justified by the fact that the *rajanya* is manifestly of Prajapati(*b*) *i.e.* of a divine origin. Without going so far that "from the dawn of the Vedic period down to the commencement of the Kautilya period, no attempt seems to have been made to divinize a ruler's person or his rights(*c*)," we might observe, that the theory of divine origin is "first hinted at in the later Vedic literature and afterwards elaborated in the Epics, Smritis and Puranas(*d*)." With the process of time, the transition has been from the human origin to the divine one, just as Hobbes' rationalizing system was

(*a*) Law, *Aspects of Ancient Indian Polity*, p. 146.

(*b*) *Sat. Brah.* V. 1, 5, 14.

(*c*) Shamasastri, *Evolution of Indian Polity*, pp. 143-4.

(*d*) P. Banerjee, *Public Administration* etc., p. 70. For divine creation of the human king, see *Indian Historical Quarterly*, Vol. I, No. 2, pp. 381-3.

followed by the works of Filmer and Bousset. In the Sutra period, no one seems to bother about the origin of kingship: it is assumed, that social order, which is the result of due observance of *swadharma*, is inconceivable without a king. The social structure of *varnasram* is eternal and the concept of *dharma* is prominent. The declaration of law is made by the Brahmins, and the king is a mere executive sovereign(*a*). The sanction for the due observance of of varna dharma and asrama dharma is to be found in the danda of the king(*b*); and the king's observance of his own peculiar dharma is enforced by moral discipline and the threat of penalty in after life. The Dharmasutras, like the Greeks, teach us, that we must consider the end for which kingship is instituted, rather than the means by which it came into being. Dharma is the offspring of Brahma and it overshadows the entire social order(*c*).

The Buddhistic theory of the origin of kingship is most remarkable, because the familiar concepts of the state of nature and contract occur in it(*d*). Naturally, kingship is a human institution, where the ideas of election and contract come in; it is more so, because of the agnosticism of the Buddhists. The stories in the various Jatakas are apt illustrations of this mode of thought. Logically, Buddhistic thought cannot sanction

(*a*) Vasistha, I, 39-41 (S. B. E. Vol. 14). Aristotelian conception of popular sovereignty is also executive and not legislative.

(*b*) The word '*danda*' occurs in Gautama, XI, 28.

(*c*) Compare *Brih. Up.* (S. B. E. Vol. 15, pp. 89-90).

(*d*) *Dighanikaya*, Aggana-Suttanta. See also Rockhill's *Life of the Buddha*, pp. 6-7.

divine origin or divine right, because, in essence, the Buddhistic movement was a stern revolt against the inequalities of the Brahminic system and the Buddhist Dhamma-chakka cannot but be founded on principles of justice, equality and brotherhood. The nature of kingship in Aryadeva's *Chatuhsatika*(*a*) follows logically from the story of Mahasammata in the Digha-nikaya. The Buddhistic theory is both realistic and rationalistic.

In the Kautilyan Arthasastra the tradition of matsyanyaya and the election of Vaivasvata Manu is referred to, but Kautilya himself seems nowhere anxious to give us an account of the origin of kingship(*b*).

This reference to matsyanyaya and the election of Manu in the Arthasastra is in the nature of a parenthesis, for the passage occurs in the speech of a spy. We cannot assume that it is the view of Kautilya, and hence cannot say with Bottazi(*c*) that the Arthasastra makes the king elective or that the sacredness of the king is "due to the power conferred on him by the people who possess in him the one defence of their existence." On the same ground, we cannot accept the view(*d*) that " Kautilya *adopted* the current idea of the king's divine nature." At best we can say, that

(*a*) Ghoshal, *Hindu Political Theories*, p. 209. See *Baudhayan*, I, 10, 1.

(*b*) See *Indian Historical Quarterly*, Dec. 1925, article, *Hindu Politics in Italian*, pp. 743-4 by Benoy K. Sarkar.

(*c*) *Indian Historical Quarterly*, Vol. I, No. 3, p. 560.

(*d*) See the footnote, pp. 137-8, *Hindu Political Theories*, Ghoshal. Here is a case of equivalence of functions, but Ghoshal confuses it with *divine nature*.

in a very old book we come across a democratic background in the institution of kingship and that the notion is put forward in such a way as to suggest its common acceptance, though not necessarily by the author. Had Kautilya been anxious to put forward a theory of the origin of kingship, surely he would have been the last person to choose chapter XIII of Book I; if he was so minded, he could have easily written something about that point in ch. IV and V in Bk. I. Assuming for the sake of argument that the view put forward is that of Kautilya, we cannot see how that passage yields the theory of king's divine nature as is assumed by Ghoshal. At best it is a case of equivalence of Indra's and Yama's functions. There is a democratic background no doubt, but it would be going too far to accept the view of Bottazi(*a*) that the passage embodies a complete theory of social contract, and that the sacredness is due to popular authority. The contract, which is rather implied, is governmental and not social. But the violation of the agreement on either side is visited, not with temporal, but, with spiritual sanctions. In our view, the passage seems to suggest a harmonious blending of two apparently opposed conceptions: a democratic background culminating in a monarchy(*b*); a human and elective origin of kingship culminating in the equivalence of king's functions with those of Indra and Yama, the two deities; a contract, in which on one side, is the entity,

(*a*) *Indian Hist. Quarterly*, ibid.

(*b*) Compare Hobbes' view. Hobbes utilises the concept of contract for justifying an absolutism. Ghoshal seems to have made a mistake in thinking otherwise. See p. 276.

called 'people', and on the other, the super-human Manu; and a secular contract, implied though it might be, coupled with spiritual sanctions. In short, it is a most remarkable blend, and kingship is here sought to be justified on grounds of contract and utility.

But when we come to Manu and Mahabharat, a different theory confronts us. In both, there is a reference to the antecedent state of nature, no doubt; but whereas in the Dighanikaya, kingship is the result of popular election and hence human in origin, in the Mahabharat and the Manava-dharmasastra it is stated to be of divine origin and consequently, the right to rule is deduced from the king's divine nature. "When these creatures," says Manu, "being without a king, through fear dispersed in all directions, the Lord created a king for the protection of the world, taking (for that purpose) eternal particles of Indra, of Anila, of Yama, of Arka, of Agni, of Varuna, of Chandra and of Kuvera." This is in connection with the king's origin. He surpasses all created beings in lustre and hence he is superior to all, because he has been formed of particles of eight deities. Even an infant king must not be despised from the idea that he is a mere mortal, for he is a great deity in human form(*a*). So Bishop Bossuet of France maintained that it was wholly wrong to look upon the king as a mere man; he was, in fact, an image of the majesty of God himself. But Bossuet goes further when he says, that open impiety on the part of a prince does not exempt the subjects from the obedience which

(*a*) *Manu*, VII, 4-8; compare *Santiparva*, sec. 68, sl. 40-41. Here 5 deities are mentioned.

they owe to him(*a*). This sort of absolutism, run mad, is not to be met with in Manu; for danda, the offspring of Brahma and a double-edged dagger, will surely destroy an autocratic and oppressive king(*b*). It is significant that the sanction does not come from the subjects. Again, Bossuet's king is *morally* bound to conform to the laws; so in Manu *dharma* is described as the son of Brahma and hence probably superior to the king, who has been made out of the particles of eight deities.

In the Mahabharat, the origin of kingship is divine no doubt(*c*), but this divine aspect is considerably modified, when we find the oppressive King Vena being killed by the rishis, and Prithu solemnly taking a coronation-oath before the assembled rishis and the gods. It is to be noted, that when confusion set in, it was the *gods* who approached the grandsire for protection and the grandsire Brahma composed the Dandaniti. But obviously, without someone who will carry into effect the principles inculcated in that treatise, the treatise by itself could not be of much help. Hence Vishnu was approached by the *gods* and the result was the institution of kingship. The divine Vishnu entered the body of Prithu and hence the entire universe offered divine worship unto Prithu numbered among human gods(*d*).

(*a*) Dunning, *Political Theories*, pp. 328-9 (From Luther to Montesquieu). Compare Narada's idea of kingship.

(*b*) VII 27.

(*c*) *Santiparva*, sec. 59; Sec. 65, sl. 30.

(*d*) *Ibid*, sl. 128. 'In a famous Bengal Vaisnava work of the early 17th century a Hindu officer of the Moslem Court is represented quite naturally as addressing his master, an unconsecrated Yavana, as a part of Vishnu.' *Ind. Hist. Quat*, Vol. I, No 2, p. 384.

The right to exact obedience from the subjects is sought to be ascribed to his divinity(*a*), and it is because the king is "really a portion of Vishnu on earth" and "has been established by the gods" that no one transcends him. "It is for this reason that everybody acts in obedience to one, and it is for this that the world cannot command him," though "belonging to the same world" and "possessed of similar limbs(*b*)." The king in the Santiparva assumes five different forms according to five different occasions. He becomes Agni, Aditya, Mrityu, Vaisravana and Yama(*c*). But underlying all these things is the idea that divinity belongs rather to the *kingly office* than to the person of the king, and this high office is a divinely-ordained duty, rather than a right bestowed from on high. For otherwise, how can we explain the fact, that an unrighteous king deserves to be slain by his subjects(*d*), and that he actually descends into hell(*e*). That kingship is a duty and not a right, is evident when Utatthya said unto Mandhatri that "one becomes a king for acting in the interest of righteousness and not for conducting himself capriciously(*f*)".

In Manu, the remedy for oppression and unrighteousness on the part of a king, is to be sought, not in the people, but in that mysterious danda. Authority from above is the principle of Manu; hence redress can not be from below. In the Mahabharat the *raison*

(*a*) *Ibid*, sloka 131. (*b*) *Ibid*, sl. 134-36.
(*c*) *Santi*, sec. 68, sl. 41. (*d*) *Santi*, sec, 92.
(*e*) *Santi*, sec. 90, sl. 4.
(*f*) *Ibid*, sl. 3. The aspect of duty is prominent in many places.

d'etre of kingship is to be found in the fact that without a king the very existence of the social order is at stake. But in order to emphasise the principle of authority and hence the majesty of the king, Vishnu has been laid under contribution. But as we have said before, the divine origin or right is considerably modified in the Santiparva, and so the redress for royal misgovernment often comes from below. The Santiparva is an amalgam of canonical and secular politics and hence this distinction between good kings and tyrants, the talk about deposition and tyrannicide, and divine origin tempered by the coronation-oath of Prithu and the inculcation of the duty of submission on the part of the subjects under pain of spiritual sanction(*a*). In fact, a theoretical justification of royal absolutism unrestrained by moral checks is nowhere to be met with except in Narada, who inculcates the doctrine of passive obedience, on the part of the subjects, in its extreme form, when he says that a ruler, though worthless, must be constantly worshipped by his subjects in the same way as a husband, though feeble, is worshipped by his wives(*b*). With the solitary exception above noted, our philosophers, even though they might sometimes advocate divine origin, do not advocate divine right to rule and misgovern and hence do not sail in the same boat with James I(*c*) and Calvin. In the opinion of Calvin(*d*),

(*a*) *Sāntiparva,* sec. 65, sl. 25-9. (*b*) *Narada*, XVIII, 22.

(c) The *True Law of Free Monarchy* seeks to substantiate that kings rule by divine right and that subjects have no recourse against them ; see Masterman, *Hist. of British Constitution* pp. 105-7.

(*d*) Dunning *Political Theories*, pp. 29-30 (From Luther to Montesquieu)

kings unworthy of all honour are to receive respectful obedience from their objects. Such is not surely the view of the author of Santiparva. Again, when Calvin says that the business of the subject is to do his duty and to leave to God the punishment of kings who fail to do their duty—well, all this sounds like canonical Hindu politics. But in the Mahabharat the doctrine of submission is tempered by the recognition of the right of tyrannicide. In short, the theory in the Mahabharat is a theory of divine origin rather than that of divine right. The theory has been further qualified, because *kingship* is of divine origin and not kings(*a*). Of course it can be argued on the basis of Vishnu's entering the body of Prithu that kings are of divine origin, but this proposition ought to be modified in view of the following facts. The very institution of kingship is created by Vishnu first of all. In the other story(*b*) though in one place(*c*) it is said, that 'gods created kings for protecting the people,' yet the initiative for the institution of kingship comes from the people and Brahma only selects Manu. In the Vena story, Narayan created Virajas, but both this Virajas and his son Krittimat did not desire sovereignty. Afterwards came Kardama, Ananga and Ativala. Now Vena was the son of this Ativala. Therefore we see that this Vena was a lineal descendant of Narayana and yet an unrighteous and oppressive king. Hence the rishis slew Vena. So far our contention is on firm

(*a*) The story of Vena and Prithu proves this.
(*b*) *Santiparva*, sec. 67, sl. 20-32.
(*c*) *Ibid*, sl. 15.

ground that *kingship* is divine and not the person of the king; otherwise why should Vena be killed. It is only in connection with Prithu, the son of Vena, that the statement has been made that Vishnu entered his body. But then it should be remembered that before being installed as a king, Prithu is made to take an oath which very much looks like a governmental compact. The divinity in the person of a king is thus very much modified, because the coronation oath comes first and then the entering of Vishnu. It is also significant that gods and rishis only are present when Prithu takes the oath and again Prithu swears to the effect that the Brahmins will be exempt from punishment(*a*). When the Brahmins have secured their rights as a result of this compact, it is only then that the person of the king becomes divine and thus the institution of kingship is put on a firmer ground. It should be noticed again that the functions of the king are sometimes equated with the functions of particular deities, and hence there is no question of divinity residing in the person of the king. Again, even if the king's person is divine, still the king has got limitations and these limitations are the limitations in consequence of the duties attached to the office of kingship(*b*). Whenever the king transgresses those limits, his divine origin and nature can no longer save him and he becomes accountable, not to God only as James I would say, but to the people also.

In the Puranas, the tradition of Manu rather than

(*a*) Sec. 59, sl. 100-110.
(*b*) Law, *Aspects* etc. p. 147.

that of Mahabharat is followed. In the *Kamandaka Nitisara* the reference to divine origin in the very first chapter is rather in the nature of a by-the-way, and Kamandaka follows his master Kautilya in his traditions. Both are interested, not in evolving a rational theory of kingship, but, in formulating principles and precepts in the just governance and expansion of a kingdom. In Kautilya's time, the contractual theory —specially in the form of a governmental compact —was much in the air, and hence Kautilya refers to it, not necessarily adopting it as a theory of his own. In the passage concerned, there is also a brief reference to the equivalence of kingly functions with the functions of two deities. Again, in the time of Kamandaka(*a*) the divine origin was probably in the air and the influence of Manu and Mahabharat may be seen in Kamandaka in that brief incidental reference. In *Sukraniti*, the brief reference to Brahma, much in the same strain as Kamandaka, is diluted by the fact, that in the very same passage(*b*) the king has been made a servant by Brahma, getting the revenue as his wages. The fact is that though Sukra mentions the name of Manu in his book, yet the standpoint of his treatise is more like that of the Arthasastras than that of the Dharmasastras of which Manava is the most important. And the divine right or origin is set at nought when Sukra declares(*c*)

(*a*) 400 A. D.—600 A.D.

(*b*) *Sacred Books of the Hindus*, Vol. 13, I, 375. For further explanation on this point, see my article, *The Arthasastra of K. and the Nitisastra of S.*

(*c*) Ibid. 363-4.

that the king is honoured because of his qualities and not because of his birth. Here the justification of king's authority rests not on his divine origin, but on utilitarian ground.

Thus we see, that the Hindu view is sometimes in favour of a human origin, sometimes in favour of a divine one and again in favour of an origin which is the resultant(*a*) of the two. Often the equivalence with the deities(*b*) is merely metaphorical and only serves to explain the different functions of the king. Sometimes the king is of the lineage of God, like the Pharaohs, as when Prithu is said to be the eighth from Vishnu(*c*). This also can be viewed as merely metaphorical, since the king is the sole protector of life and property in this earth, just as Vishnu is said to be the protector of the entire universe ; and hence it is but logical, that the king is 'really a portion of Vishnu on earth.' Sometimes the notion is, that the institution of kingship is divine, but not necessarily the king himself. In Manu, both the notions are prominent. Even if kings be of divine origin, it is rarely that he rules by divine right ; for there are the twin concepts of dharma and danda, the latter in an abstract sense, placed over the king. When it is a case of divine origin, the concept of duty on the part of the king is prominent and rajadharma sections of the Dharmasastras illustrate that. Sovereignty when

(*a*) *Santiparva.*
(*b*) *Sukraniti*, ch I ; *Santiparva*, sec. 68 ; *Arthasastra*, I, 13 ; *Kamandakaniti*, III, 1.
(*c*) *Santi*, sec. 59, sl. 112. The Scythian innovation of king as *Devaputra* is said to be of Chinese origin. See *Cal. Review*, Sept. 1925, pp. 479-80.

viewed as a thing of divine origin, is a matter rather of duty than of right and this line of thought is first evident in the writings of the canonical school, according to whom Politics is a part of practical ethics. At one end of the scale, there is the human conception carried to its logical extreme in the Jataka stories ; at the other end, are the Pharaoh-like conception of Prithu as the eighth from Vishnu and its logical corollary, the doctrine of passive obedience enunciated by Narada. Between these two extremes(*a*), there are degrees of humanity and divinity, and even deities in Hindu pantheon are subject to duties and limitations and amenable to spiritual, if not temporal, sanctions. The simple generalisation of Willoughby(*b*), that 'in all of the vast Asiatic monarchies of early days the rulers claimed a divine right to control the affairs of the state and this was submitted to by the people with but little question' should be assessed at its proper value.

(*a*) Indra's sovereignty is sometimes due to *election* by gods, sometimes derived from the *will of god*. It is a case of authority from below or above. *Hindu Political Theories*. pp. 42-3.

(*b*) *Nature of the State*, pp. 42-3.

APPENDIX

The development in the order of thought—how a human origin of kingship tends to move towards a divine one—might be illustrated thus :—

(1) Human Origin :—

(a) external pressure, e.g. war. (Ait. Brah.)

(b) internal necessity, contract. (Dighanikaya)

(2) Human Origin + Invocation to deities; election supplemented by prayer. (Sat. Brah.; for Abhishechaniyam see 'Hindu Polity', II, 23)

(3) Equivalence of functions. (Mahabharat, Santi; Sukraniti)

(4) Temporary divinity during sacrifice. (Vajapeya and Rajasuya sacrifices)

(5) Human form + Particles of several deities. (Manu; Sukraniti)

(6) Descendant of God. (Prithu, eighth from Vishnu; Vishnu enters his body, Santiparva)

(7) Kingship is divine, but not the person of the king. (Story of Vena. Sukraniti and Kamandakaniti might be interpreted in this way)

CHECKS TO TYRANNY IN HINDU POLITICAL THOUGHT

An attempt will be made here to enumerate and describe the different forms of checks to tyranny, which the writers on ancient Indian politics assumed as essential adjuncts in their systems of political thought. We shall mainly concentrate our attention to the doctrines of checks and resistance; but, shall, where possible, refer to actual facts. Moreover, when enumerating these checks, it need not be taken for granted, as a matter of course, that they had an existence in the objective world(*a*). In short, our main concern is with the subjective aspect.

There is an idea abroad, especially among the Europeans and the Americans, that the most important category of political thought among the ancient

(*a*) Dr. Pramathanath Banerjee's *Public Administration in Ancient India*—a very good account of the systems of public administration visualised by diverse writers on politics—is vitiated by the author's failure to keep this distinction in view. Referring to "some of the shortcomings which characterize a great deal of these magazine articles and books" Prof. Benoy Kumar Sarkar remarks—"the distinction between the institution of *Realpolitik* and the "pious wishes" or ideals of theorizers has virtually been neglected or ignored." See p. 7 of his *Positive Background of Hindu Sociology* Bk. II, Part I. Prof. Jadunath Sarkar neglects the "subjective" aspect entirely. See his *Studies in Mughal India* pp. 304-10.

Hindus is an unfettered kingship, an undisguised tyranny. The truth is exactly the reverse. If unfetterred kingship had been one of the postulates of political thought amongst the writers on Hindu politics, surely the doctrine of passive obedience(*a*) would have loomed large in the pages of the Dharmasastras and the Arthasastras of old. The doctrine of passive obedience implies, not only that the subjects are to implicitly obey their king, but that they must not think of resisting an impious and oppressive ruler. In fact, this doctrine, in its most obnoxious and extreme form, is scarcely to be met with in the political literature of ancient India(*b*).

The checks, which are contemplated by ancient Hindu writers, and examples of which are to be found scatterred in the various *Dharmasastras*, *Arthasastras*, *Puranas*, *Nitisastras* and epics, may be broadly classified under two heads, *viz.*, preventive and retributive. Preventive checks may be defined as checks which by their very nature tend to prevent a king from degenerating into a tyrant. By retributive checks kings are punished for wrongs committed by them: there is an element of retribution in the latter kind of checks. These checks are, on a final analysis, sufficiently preventive in their nature. By their examples, future incumbents in the office of kingship were prevented from perpetrating wrongs. Preventive checks

(*a*) But see *Narada*, S. B. E. XVIII, 21.

(*b*) "As a husband, though feeble, must be constantly worshipped by his wives, in the same way, a ruler, though worthless, must be (constantly) worshipped by his subjects." S. B. E. XVIII, 22, *Narada*.

may be subdivided into internal preventive checks and external preventive checks. These external preventive checks may again be classified under two heads, *viz.*, religious and political. Retributive checks are of three kinds, *viz.*, fines, deposition and tyrannicide. Here is the classification :—

- Checks
  - Preventive
    - Internal
    - External
      - Religious
      - Political
  - Retributive
    - Fines
    - Deposition
    - Tyrannicide

" During the period of studentship, the prince has to live the austere life of a Brahmachari, observing celibaey and undergoing the hardships involved in the study of the different subjects(*a*)". Kautilya(*b*) lays great stress on the restraint of the organs of sense on the part of a king by abandoning lust, anger, greed, vanity, haughtiness and overjoy. Sukracharjya considers, that ' discipline is the chief thing to the king(*c*),' and that ' the king should first provide discipline to himself, then to the sons, then to ministers, then to servants, then to the subjects(*d*)'. In fact, the ancient

(*a*) *Aspects of Ancient Indian Polity*, Narendranath Law, p. 72, see ch. V.

(*b*) I, 5-6.

(*c*) *Sukraniti*, (B. K. Sarkar) I, 181-2.

(*d*) *Ibid.* 183-5.

Hindu writers on politics cannot conceive of a king who has not got this moral training. Manu is of opinion, that the king should possess knowledge of his own self. For our purposes, the importance of this moral discipline as a most effective check to tyranny is patent; since a king who has conquered his senses is not likely to degenerate into a tyrant. A check which acts from within, is more effective than one which acts from outside; and it is from this point of view, perhaps, that the ancient Hindus preferred the internal preventive checks to the legal and constitutional checks, so dear to the heart of a moderner. A king who has abandoned greed, is not likely to make illegal exactions and thereby become a tyrant, and need not die like 'Aila in his attempt under the influence of greed to make exactions from Brahmins, as well as Ajabindu the Sauvira (in a similar attempt)(*a*). To a student of politics in the 20th century familiar with all the apparatuses of democratic government, the importance, which the Hindus attached to moral discipline on the part of a king, may seem queer and well-nigh grotesque; but in ancient India when democratic government on on a big scale was unknown; when the king, both of the rajadharma and the arthasastra school, was the mainspring of the whole mechanism; and kingship was looked upon as a sacred trust; the importance of this moral discipline(*b*) to the body politic cannot be overestimated. "Yet I am inclined to believe that such

(*a*) *Arthasastra*, I, 6. Cupidity of Rajarshi Aila is also mentioned in *Sukraniti*, I, 287-90.

(*b*) Hence the Hindu ideal of kingship was a Rajarshi one for the rajadharma school.

religious and moral restraints, as self-denial, conquest of the six passions, preparation for Moksha or Nirvana by renunciation, frequently preached to the prince and poor alike, were scarcely less powerful than the constitutional and legal checks of western nations of modern times. How far the modern constitutional checks, based more on utilitarian than ethical principles, are preferable to religious or philosophical restraints, which are applicable to all, is a question yet to be decided(*a*)".

The second class of preventive checks which were religious in their nature was effective in as much as they took advantage of the religious beliefs and prejudices of the age. But it must be remembered, that it was the Dharmasastras, more than the Arthasastras, that utilised this class of checks,—obviously for the reason, that the standpoint of the Arthasastras was secular. Manu says, "A king who (duly) protects (his subjects) receives from each and all the sixth part of their spiritual merit ; if he does not protect them, the sixth part of their demerit also (will fall on him)(*b*)" ; and again, "A king who does not afford protection, (yet) takes his share in kind * * * * will (after death) soon sink into hell(*c*)." In the Agni Purana also, we find that an oppressive king lives in hell for all time to come. Sukra ordains hell(*d*) or the condition of lower animals(*e*) for *tamasa* kings. Kautilya,

(*a*) Shamasastri, *Evolution of Indian Polity*, preface, xiv.

(*b*) *Manu*, VIII, 304, S. B. E.

(*c*) *Manu*, VIII, 307.

(*d*) *Sukraniti*, I, 63, 171.

(*e*) *Ibid*, I, 64-8.

who treats politics from a secular standpoint, is not free from this religious touch, because, "the king who guides his subjects in accordance with the above rules will attain to heaven ; otherwise he will fall into the hell(*a*)". In the insertion of dialogues amongst the spies the kings are made answerable for the sins of their subjects, when the principle of levying just punishments and taxes has been violated(*b*).

The prospect of hell for a modern tyrant will not in the least dissuade him from his career of tyranny ; such a check is sure to evoke a peal of laughter from a modern audience ; but its utility in ancient times cannot for a moment be questioned, when we remember, that the mass, not excluding the king, really believed in heaven and hell.

The "political-preventive" checks are Laws and Customs, Public Opinion, Ministers and Assemblies. In ancient India, the legislative sovereignty of the kings was rather limited ; the only sovereignty which they exercised was rather executive in its nature(*c*). The rules of socio-religious conduct were laid down in the Srutis and Smritis, and the king only administered them. Besides these, custom was not to be neglected, even if it conflicted with the current ideas of morality.

(*a*) *Artha*, III, 7.

(*b*) *Arthasastra*, I, 13.

(*c*) *Calcutta Weekly Notes*, Vol. 15, pp. xxii-xxiv. See Naresh Sen Gupta, *Sources of Law and Society in Ancient India*, pp. 78-81. It might also be pointed out that Greek laws were "revealed," and that the Greek conception of sovereignty was also executive, but see Barker, *Greek Political Theory*: *Pluto and his Predecessors* pp. 295-6. See Benoy Sarkar, *Pol. Institutions*, etc. ch. 4, sec. 5 and ch. 9, sec. 2 (b)

The sphere of king's legislative power was still further circumscribed by the laws and customs observed by the various corporations, social and economic(*a*). Local customs, however objectionable, must be maintained, 'for otherwise the people get agitated(*b*)'. According to Kautilya(*c*), *Dharma*, *Vyabahara*, *Charitra* and *Rajasasana* are the four legs of law. The Dharmasastras hold that the king is not above law ; but according to Kautilya(*d*), king's law is the most authoritative, and when in conflict with the sacred law, the king's law will be obeyed. But lest it should be thought, that this supreme law-making power of the king means, in effect, absolutism, the Sukraniti lays down(*e*), that the king should administer *nyaya* in the noon and Smriti in the morning. Sukra's *nyaya* is possibly the *dharma-nyaya*(*f*) of Kautilya, which is nothing but king-made law. The Mahabharat(*g*) also lays down, that "if the king transgresses all wholesome restraints, all people become filled with alarm.** For this reason, the king should always establish rules and restraints for gladdening the hearts of his people. Rules in respect of even very trivial matters are hailed with delight by the people". The implication of all these quotations is that government by law, even if made by the king, is preferable to government by executive fiats. Kautilya's assertion, that the king-

(*a*) *Sukraniti*, IV-V, 89-93.

(*b*) For an account of these customs viz. beef-eating, sexual immorality, etc. see Sukra.

(*c*) *Artha*, III, 1. (*d*) *Ibid.*

(*e*) IV-V 106. (*f*) *Artha*, III, 1.

(*g*) *Santiparva*, sec. 133.

made law or Rajasasana is the most authoritative, points to the fact, that the Maurjya kings were law-making sovereigns; whereas the insistence of the Dharmasastrakaras(*a*), on kings being subordinate to dharma, points to the kings being executive sovereigns. In the first case, king-made laws and customs were the checks; in the second case, customs and Dharmasastras as interpreted by a *Parsad*(*b*).

The strength of public opinion may be gauged by the dictum, which Sukra lays down, that a king 'should dismiss the officer who is accused by one hundred men(*c*)'. This theory of ministerial responsibility and king's irresponsibility is hinted at in the drama Mudra-Rakshasa(*d*), where it is said, "when anything wrong is done by the king, the fault is of the minister; (for) it is through the negligence of the driver, that an elephant goes mad." That the ministers and officers of the king were sensitive to public opinion may be illustrated by the story told by Hiuen Tsang about Vikramaditya, king of Sravasti. The king ordered his officers to distribute daily five lakhs of gold coins. The officer in charge of the revenues mildly protested, saying, that such indiscriminate charity would entail fresh taxation, for which the ministers would be blamed by the people(*e*). Sukra's dictum, about the dismissal by king of officers accused by one hundred men, is nothing but the

(*a*) Exception will be noted later on.

(*b*) *Yagnabalka Smriti* (S. B. H. Vol. 21, sutra 9).

(*c*) *Sukra*, I, 755. (*d*) Act III, quoted, Pramatha Banerjee.

(*e*) Beal, *Buddhist Records*, Bk II, quoted Banerjee.

'doctrine of recall in embryo' as Benoy Kumar Sarkar puts it(*a*). Sukra also emphasises that 'the wise ruler should ever abide by the well-thought-out decisions of councillors, office-bearers, *subjects and members attending a meeting*—never by his own opinions(*b*)'. In another passage, he lays it down, that 'the unity of opinion possessed by the many is more powerful than the king. The rope that is made by a combination of many threads is strong enough to drag the lion(*c*)'. In order to illustrate the strength of public opinion we may cite the story of Devapi and Santanu. Devapi, the eldest son of the king, was a leper; but the king decided to instal him as heir-apparent. The people opposed the king, who ultimately had to change his decision. Again, when Yayati decided to instal Puru, his youngest son, as his heir, the citizens objected to Puru on the ground of his being the youngest; but the king succeeded in convincing the people by saying that all his other sons are disobedient and as such are no sons. Here the king had to justify his seemingly autocratic action to the citizens.

But the real and the most effective 'political-preventive' checks were the ministers and assemblies. In the Vedic period, the assembly and the king were the two important elements that constituted the government, and of these two, surely the assembly possessed the greater political power, as is evident from the various hymns of the Atharva-veda con-

(*a*) *Positive Background of Hindu Sociology, Political*, p. 43.

(*b*) *Sukra*, II, 5-6. (*c*) *Ibid*, IV-VII, 838-9.

cerning banishment and restoration of kings. The Vedic monarchy was sometimes elective and sometimes hereditary. During the periods of interregnum due to death or banishment of kings, it was the assembly that managed the affairs of a kingdom(*a*). 'While during the Vedic period the assembly evidently held a permanent place in the constitution, it occupied a subordinate place in the Sutra period(*b*)'. With the increase of the territory of the state, the growth of the king's power and the rigidity of the caste system, the popular assembly gradually ceased to function, and it was physically impossible to gather all the citizens of a big state at a fixed time and place(*c*). But it must not be understood, that with the gradual decay of the Sabhas and Samitis, disappeared all wholesome checks upon king's arbitrary use of power. The place of assembly in the system of government was taken up by the ministry.

The importance of the ministry as an indispensable organ of the state has been recognized by all the writers on politics. Kautilya referring to the ministers says, "A single wheel can never move. Hence he (king) shall employ ministers and hear their opinion(*d*).

(*a*) *Evolution of Indian Polity*, p. 87.

(*b*) *Ibid.*

(*c*) So as Rome grew, democracy gave way. The difficulty in those days was that the representative system was unknown.

(*d*) *Artha*, I, 7. In the *Matsya Purana* the first duty of a king on ascending the throne is to "pick out worthy men for his assembly as his advisers," since the 'smallest function cannot successfully be performed by one single man'. Ch. 215 (S. B. H.)

Speaking of the appointment of the high-priest, Kautilya says, "As a student his teacher, a son his father, and a servant his master, the king shall follow him(*a*)'. Now this high priest had important 'spiritual and religious duties that gave him influence over the monarch, not only in domestic and religious, but also in all important secular matters, including public and political questions(*b*)'. That the ministers were supposed to be real checks upon the king is evident from Sukra's query, 'can there be prosperity of the kingdom, if there be ministers whom the ruler does not fear(*c*)?' And also 'if the king fears their control, they are good ministers(*d*)'. Sukra, speaking of subservient ministers, says, that they ought 'to be gratified like women with decorations, liveries of honour etc(*e*)'—thus showing his contempt for them. That the king must not be self-willed, must 'abide by the well-thought-out decisions of councillors' are proof positive of the fact, that the ministers played an equal, if not more important, part in the administration of the state. It has been shown also that the ministers recognised some responsibility to the people(*f*), and thus we see that the ministers were never taken as so many creatures of the king. In fact, such a system of government can be aptly described as *Sachivatantra*—as Pramathanath Banerjee puts it(*g*)—or *Minis-*

(*a*) *Ibid*, I, 9.
(*b*) Law, *Ancient Indian Polity*, pp. 38-9. "The didactic parts of the Mahabharat recommend complete dependence of the sovereign upon his Purohita," p. 49.
(*c*) II, 164. (*d*) *Ibid*, 163. (*e*) *Ibid*, 165.
(*f*) Story of Vikramaditya told by Hiuen Tsang.
(*g*) *Pub. Adm.* p. 51.

trocracy if we are allowed to say so. In Mudra-Rakshasa we find the term 'Sachivayatta-tantra,' that is to say, a form of government, in which real power exists in the hands of the ministers(*a*). In the ancient kingdoms of Chera, Chola and Pandya there were five assemblies associated with the king in the administration of the state. Of these five, surely the assembly of the people and the assembly of the ministers were the most important, because the former looked after the rights and privileges of the people, while the latter attended to the general administration of the state. Such a system of constitutional monarchy, not as a speculative theory, but as an objective reality, may appear unique in ancient Indian polity, but Kanaksabhai is of opinion, that this form of government was not peculiar to South India, but had its original in the Magadhan Empire of the north. Kautilya also speaks of the minister as installing the heir-apparent and also of his investing himself with the powers of sovereignty(*b*). A glimpse of the ministerial authority may also be got, when after the assassination of Rajyavardhana, the Prime Minister proposed in an assembly of ministers, that Harshavardhana should ascend the throne. Just as the assembly in the Vedic period managed the affairs

(*a*) Quoted, Pramatha Banerjee, *Public Adm.* In the Jatakas we also find religious-minded kings handing over kingly powers to the ministers. "Decision regarding succession to the throne was often left to the ministers. We also find mention of actual exercise of sovereignty by the ministers."—Fick, *Social Organisation* (*Eng. Trans*), p. 140.

(*b*) *Artha*, V, 6.

of the kingdom during the periods of interregnum, due to death or banishment of kings, so the ministers of the kingdom of Ceylon after the death of Vijaya, took over the administration in their own hands, until they invested a new king with the powers of sovereignty(*a*). Thus we see, that often the right to sovereignty was granted by the ministers—a fact, whose implications ought not to be lost sight of(*b*). One of these implications is, that if the ministers can make a king, they can unmake also, and so we find that Lilavati who was elected Queen of Ceylon by the ministers was afterwards deposed by them(*c*). That the government of Queen Lilavati was a constitutional monarchy, is evident from an inscription of Lilavati where she says: 'By creating a Council of wise, brave and faithful ministers, she has freed her own kingdom from the dangers (arising) from other kingdoms'. The doctrine enunciated in Mudra-Rakshasa—that when anything wrong is done by the king, the fault is of the minister—is reasonable, if the king is bound to accept the advice tendered by his ministers; and hence we find, that 'the king, who does not listen to the counsels of ministers about things good and bad to him, is a thief in the form of a ruler, an exploiter of the people's wealth' (*d*) and 'soon gets estranged from his kingdom and alienated with his subjects(*e*).'

(*a*) *Mahavamsa*; Cf. the Rajakrits or kingmakers in Atharva-Veda and *Satapath Brahman.*

(*b*) In England from the time of William III, the right to throne depends on Parliamentary title.

(*c*) *Public Adm.* p. 117. (*d*) *Sukraniti*, II, 515-16.

(*e*) *Ibid*, 7-8—on the subject of ministry, see R. G. Basak, *Ministers in Ancient India*; *Ind. Historical Quarterly*, Vol. I, No. 3-4, 1925.

So far we have dealt with preventive checks ; now we shall consider retributive checks.

That the kings had to pay fines, when they committed offences, is evident from the following quotation from Manu,—'where another common man would be fined one karshapana, the king shall be fined one thousand (*a*).'

In the Vedic period, the assembly seems to have had powers 'to degrade a king to the rank of the common people or of the clan of nobles(*b*)'—evidently for some wrongs committed by kings.

The Atmamedha or Prayopavesa form of passive resistance—a vow of abstinence to death on the part of the people *en masse*, till the removal of the cause of their grievances, seems to have been a very potent weapon in the hands of the oppressed citizens against their tyrannical rulers. Shamasastri is of opinion, 'that the Atmamedha form of passive resistance was invented by the Vedic poets to check the licentious proceedings of some of their Asura kings(*c*).' This kind of check is both preventive and retributive. It is preventive, in that it is resorted to to compel a king to change his unjust attitude, and to reclaim a king from his wicked habits. 'From Rajatarangini VI, 14, it appears, that ancient kings used to send spies to find out and report voluntary cases of prayopavesa or

(*a*) S. B. E. Vol. 25, 336. 'When the king punishes an innocent man, he shall throw into water dedicating to God Varuna a *fine* equal to thirty times the unjust imposition.' *Arthasastra*, IV, 13.

(*b*) *Evolution of Indian Polity*, Appendix A.

(*c*) *Ibid*, Appendix B. Cf. Mahatma Gandhi's conception of passive resistance.

fasting to death, and to redress such grievances as were the causes of these long fasts(*a*).' Some element of retribution is also involved in this check, in as much as a tyrannical king was regarded as the indirect murderer of those citizens resorting to starvation by death ; and the enormity of such a crime to a Hindu, well-versed in the ancient traditions, can very well be imagined. Perhaps, such a king gets the condition of lower animals after death. This form of check was also used to expel a tyrannical king(*b*).

The idea of deposition and tyrannicide is not wholly repugnant to the Hindus. In the Vedic period, when kings were regarded as mere mortals, and when monarchy was generally elective and people's assembly had the upper hand, it is not surprising that kings were often expelled. We know that 'Dustaritu Paumsayana had been expelled from the kingdom which had come down to him through ten generations and the Sringayas also expelled Revottaras Patava Kakra-Sthapati(*c*)'. In the Arthasastra of Kautilya, we do not come across any enunciation of the right or duty of deposition and tyrannicide, though Kautilya views Arthasastra wholly from a secular and utilitarian aspect. Notwith standing this, the idea of deposition or tyrannicide is not unknown, for Kautilya lays down as a matter of common knowledge, that 'a king of unrighteous character and of vicious habits will, though he is an emperor, fall a prey either to the fury of his own subjects or to

(*a*) *Ibid.*

(*b*) *Taitteriya Samhita* II. 3, 1—Quoted by Shamasastri. The atmamedha form of check has not been shown in the classification, because it is difficult to classify it.

(*c*) S. B. E. Vol. XLIV, p. 269.

that of his enemies(*a*)'. In another place(*b*) he tells us that impoverished, greedy and disaffected subjects voluntarily destroy their own master. In the chapter on Purity or Impurity in the character of ministers, one spy is made to say, "this king is unrighteous; well, let us set up in his place another king who is righteous(*c*)". Later on in the same chapter, another spy is made to say, 'the king has betaken himself to an unwise course; well, having murdered him, let us put another in his stead'. In this, though in an indirect way(*d*), we are confronted with a distinction between a good king and a tyrant(*e*). A king in Kautilya's view must not be so haughty as to despise all people, or, in other words, must not be tyrannical; for, if tyrannical, they are likely to perish like Dambhodbhaba and Arjuna of Haihaya dynasty(*f*).

The rajadharma section of the Santiparva in Mahabharat, which is a blend of canonical and Arthasastric ideas of politics, makes a sharp distinction between a righteous king and a tyrant(*g*). This admixture is apparent in the divine and popular origin of kingship. But it is reasonable to suppose, that its secular aspect got the upper hand, in that the Mahabharat gives no quarter to an unrighteous king. The

(*a*) *Arthasastra*, VI, 1.
(*b*) VII, 5. (*c*) I, 10.
(*d*) Because Kautilya makes the spy distingiush between a good king and a tyrant.
(*e*) Usurpers of thrones are also tyrants and hence killed. See *Matsya Purana*, Ch. 214 (S.B.H.).
(*f*) *Artha*, I, 6.
(*g*) It is curious that Upendra Nath Ghoshal makes Sukra the first originator of this distinction (*Hindu Political Theories*, p. 258) and again on p. 100 of his book gives the credit to another.

great rishi Vamadeva is quoted by Bhisma to have said, 'that king, who acts according to the counsels of a vicious and sinful minister, becomes a destroyer of righteousness and *deserves to be slain* by his subjects with all his family(*a*)', and again, 'that king who is illiberal and without affection, who afflicts his subjects by undue chastisement and who is rash in his acts, soon meets with destruction(*b*)'. In the Anusasanaparva, the subjects are advised to arm themselves for slaying the tyrant and again, the 'king, who tells his people that he is their protector, but who does not or is unable to protect them, should be slain by his *combined* subjects'. A perusal of these quotations will convince any one, that the king of Mahabharat is more a mortal than a *nara-devata* or that only a righteous king can claim the title of nara-devata(*c*). In the Aswamedhaparva, we read of one Khanikhetra deposed by his subjects(*d*). 'King Vena, a slave of wrath and malice, became unrighteous in his conduct towards all creatures. The rishis, those utterers of Brahma, slew him with *kusha* blades (as their weapon) inspired with *mantras*(*e*)'. After Vena has been killed, the rishis pierced his right arm whence sprang a person, who was annointed as king,

(*a*) *Santiparva*, sec. 92. (*b*) *Ibid.*

(*c*) See in this connection *Manu*, V, 96-7 ; VII, 4-8 ; *Sukra*, I, 139-43 ; also footnote, p. 71, of *Public Adm. in Ancient India* ; also footnote, pp. 182-3 of *Hindu Political Theories* by Upendra Nath Ghoshal. Dr. Ghoshal's view that Sukra's theory is peculiar, is not justified in view of similar opinions being held by the author of Mahabharat.

(*d*) *Carmichael Lectures*, 1918, p. 136, footnote.

(*e*) *Santiparva*, sec. 59 ; see also *Matsya Purana*, S. B. H. part I, ch. X.

after having taken an oath that he would never act with caprice and would fearlessly maintain the duties laid down in the Vedas. This looks something like a coronation-oath—the implication being that if he acts upon his whims and caprices, he will be slain outright like his father Vena. Such a coronation-oath seems to have been employed in Aindramahavi-seka ceremony when a promise was extorted from the king, that he would lose everything, *even his life*, if he attempted violation of right and truth(*a*). In the Agnipurana, it is laid down, that a tyrant is deposed and killed, sooner or later(*b*).

In the Buddhistic *Dighanikaya* we are confronted with the rudiments of social and governmental compacts(*c*), and the implications of the contractual origin of kingship are far-reaching. It means that the king is liable to popular control ; but it is to be regretted, that the implications were not systematized as part of a general theory of state(*d*). However, the loss in theory has been partly made good by instances of deposition and tyrannicide which we find in the Jatakas. In the Saccamkira Jataka(*e*), we find the wicked king of Benares, who owed his life

(*a*) *Aitareya Brahmana*, quoted by Radhakumud Mukherjee in *Fundamental Unity of India*.

(*b*) Ch. 225, 31-32, quoted by Madhusudhan Bhattacharjee in his *Ratnamala*, part I.

(*c*) The title "Mahasammata" indicates elective origin.

(*d*) For a short account of the Buddhistic theory see Ghoshal's *Hindu Political Theories*, pp. 117-123 and 209-212. The conception of king as *ganadasa* or servant of the people from the point of view of checks to tyranny must not be lost sight of.

(*e*) Vol. I, edited by Cowell.

to Bodhisatta, asking his followers to catch hold of Bodhisatta and execute him. Bodhisatta recited, how he saved the king, while he was crown-prince. "Filled with indignation at his recital, the nobles and brahmins and all classes with one accord cried out, 'This ungrateful king does not recognise even the goodness of this good man, who saved his majesty's life. How can we have any profit from this king. Seize the tyrant.' And in their anger, they rushed upon the king from every side and slew him then and there". Again in the Padakusalamanava Jataka(*a*), a king, who had himself stolen some treasures, employed a young man to specify the thief. Before a great audience, the young man said that their refuge proved their bane, whereupon the people thought, "* * * that he may not in future go on playing the part of a thief, we will kill this wicked king." So they rose up with sticks and clubs in their hands and then and there beat the king and priest till they died. In the Mahasutasoma Jataka(*b*), the citizens asked the commander to have the king expelled from his kingdom, if he would not give up his cannibalistic propensities. The commander thereupon requested the king to give it up, who however expressed his inability to comply with this request ; whereupon the commander said, "Then depart sire, from this city and kingdom." It will be evident from these stories that there was nothing divine, nothing sacred in the Buddhistic conception of kingship(*c*).

(*a*) Vol. III.
(*b*) Vol. V.
(*c*) Compare what the Buddhist monk Aryadeva says,

The distinction between a good king and a tyrant has been maintained by Sukra(*a*). According to Sukra, any and every king is not divine, or is not a *nara-devata*, because the king who is not virtuous is 'a part of the demons', and as such gets hell, or the condition of lower animals after death. But that is not enough. 'If the king be an enemy of virtue, morality and strength, people should desert (expel) him as the ruiner of the state, and in his place for the maintenance of the state, the priest with the consent of the *Prakriti*, should instal one who belongs to his family and qualified(*b*)'. Sukra cannot bear with a king, who does not listen to the counsels of his ministers(*c*), to him an autocratic king is nothing but a 'thief in the form of a ruler'. Other hints at deposition are given in some more places(*d*). It will be seen, that Sukra nowhere sanctions tyrannicide, though he says, that the king is justly looked upon as a dog by the poets(*e*), and also quotes the example of Vena being killed on account of his unrighteousness(*f*). It will be further observed, that Sukra observes a *via media*; any and every king is not a nara-devata, nor a mere mortal; that is, a virtuous king is godlike(*g*), the

"what superciliousness is thine, (O king!), thou who art a (mere) servant of the multitude (ganadasa) and who receivest the sixth part (of the produce) as thine wages".

(*a*) I, 63, 69-70, 139-40, 171.

(*b*) II, 549-52. (*c*) II, 515-6.

(*d*) I, 277-8, 279-80 ; II, 5-8 ; IV-VII, 826-9.

(*e*) I, 745-6. (*f*) I, 137-8.

(*g*) Cf. "Atri was the first to deify a king, so that Gautama called him a sycophant, but Sanatkumar upheld the deification". Quoted from Hopkins' *Epic Mythology*, p. 184.

reverse, demonlike. Further, he makes the king a creature of Brahma, but qualifies it by saying that he is a servant of the people(*a*). He sanctions deposition, a necessary corollary of the king being a servant of the people—but nowhere sanctions the extreme penalty which a tyrant deserves, *viz.*, tyrannicide. With Narada, he does not say, whatever a king does is right(*b*), nor does he support the view advocated by Aryadeva, that the king is a *mere* servant of the people and nothing more.

Yagnabalka warns the king against illegal taxation, by saying, that 'the fire, arising from the heat of the suffering of the subjects, does not cease, without fully burning the family, fortune and life of the king(*c*)'.

In the Mahavamsa, Vijaya is described as a Prince Regent whose maladministration led to discontent and ultimately to his own banishment(*d*). Again Queen Lilavati of Ceylon was deposed by her ministers(*e*).

After every thing has been said about these various kinds of checks to tyranny, a critic might reasonably put in, that in no Hindu political literature, has any theory about the rights of the people been systematically developed. To this, our answer is, that the ancient Hindus thought more in terms of Swadharma and duties, than in those of Swadhikara and rights.

(*a*) I, 375.
(*b*) S. B. E. XVIII, 21.
(*c*) Sutra 341, S. B. H. Vol. 21.
(*d*) Quoted by Pramathanath Banerjee, p. 89 footnote.
(*e*) For some historical examples of deposition see Benoy Sarkar's *Political Institutions and Theories of the Hindus*, chap. 4 sec. 7.

THE CONCEPT OF LAW AND THE EARLY HINDU VIEW

THE Austinian conception of law, following in the footsteps of Bodin and Hobbes, brought definiteness and precision in our idea of law, no doubt, but this it did by following a policy of strenuous exclusion. This policy of exclusion, which limited the scope of laws only to those rules of conduct prescribed by the sovereign body of an independent state and enforced by the physical sanction of a well-organized state, has in effect been challenged by the Historical school of jurists, who point out that rudiments of law are to be found in the primitive stages of society, in which it cannot be described as the command of a sovereign in a political society, enforced by the physical sanction of that body politic. John Austin might have said in criticism of Savigny, that the latter, when he represented law as a product of national life, was only referring to its *historical* sources ; while he, in defining law as the command of a definite political superior, was only referring to its *juridical* source. John Austin's immediate concern was to determine the scope of a lawyer's Jurisprudence, while Savigny's point of view, like Maine's, was to expound a philosophy of law(*a*). The mechanical view of law, as a fiat imposed upon the people by the sovereign body, comes in handy in the modern age, when we are confronted with the incessant activity in legislation of the modern parliaments; but the bankruptcy of this theory is evident, when we betake ourselves to the era of customary law. But both the mechanical and the organic theories of law err, because of their extreme points of view. The correct standpoint would be to regard law as a creation of the human mind and an unconscious growth at the same time; because inspite of growing social self-consciousness, there is always an element of spontaneity and instinctive habit lurking in the background.

The analysis of the Austinian conception of law into its constituent elements has not gone unchallenged. At present, the scope of the concept law has been very much enlarged.

It is said(*b*), that the notions of *sovereignty* and *command* are not essential presuppositions in the concept of law, and that all rules of conduct, imposed and enforced by society as such for the conduct of social

(*a*) The Historical treatment of law was first begun in Germany by Eichhorn. Savigny expounded this historical interpretation of law, because he was against the formulation of a new German Code. Maine was against any scheme of legislation based on first principles, because his historical method is only another name for the theory of Darwinian evolution in legal and social institutions.

Austin took cognizance of the fact that there were various kinds of social rules; but he designated them as positive morality.

(*b*) The line of criticism here adopted is that of Vinogradoff's. See his *Commonsense in Law*.

and political relations, are to be given the appellation of law. It is to be seen, that the definite human political superior of Austin is replaced by the indefinite entity called the society, and that the notion of command is too mechanical to explain the growth of laws in the customary era. Again, the notion of physical sanction of force is too crude. We cannot say, that a good citizen does not commit murder merely because there is the penal code : his abstention from murder is not to be explained by the fact of prospective punishment like death or life-long imprisonment. It might be the result of the sting of his conscience or instinctive conformity or a negative attitude of non-resistance. At best, we may say, that there is the prospective indignant public opinion which may act as a deterrent. In all this, of course, some kind of sanction is implied : whether it be the sting of one's own conscience, or the contempt or hostility of the general public ; but this sanction may be inflicted by an indeterminate human entity (as opposed to a definite tribunal), or else by a supernatural being(*a*). The fundamental background of law is provided, not by the physical sanction of force, but, by recognition or agreement, because the

(*a*) Instances are to be found in books on primitive culture. In some of the primitive societies, adultery is looked upon with horror, not because it is immoral, but because it will rouse the anger of some supernatural being, who will inflict terrible penalties upon the whole tribe. 'Ruin to the crops, continuous drought, continuous rains, are the results of incest, according to the Dayaks, the Battas, the Galelareese (who also attribute earthquake and eruptions to the same crime) and other tribes'. See *Ency. of Religion and Ethics*, Vol. 4, p. 253.

organized force employed in enforcing laws is not likely to be very much effective, unless there be, at least, tacit agreement behind the employment of force, and also a conscious or unconscious recognition of the fact that the authority of the law ought to be upheld(*a*).

The habit of falling into antithesis, so characteristic of the Sophistic way of thinking, whether as an aid in constructing a philosophy or in attacking social institutions with clever dialectic, has often been condemned by some, because it takes a too mechanical view of the object of thought. The Sophists divided all phenomena into human and natural; and with this, sought to criticise the existing human institutions. Those, who condemn this way of thinking, forget, that this method, however imperfect and illogical it may seem, serves as the best starting-point of thought, because human mind always delights in contrasting A with not-A, and this method of contrast serves to bring out the essential attributes of each. Of course, we do not deny that there is a certain amount of "sophistry" in this mode of thought, and that higher philosophy ought to take a more comprehensive view of the two sharply-divided categories of phenomena by treating them as exhibiting differences in degree only; but it is to be noted that both(*b*) Mill and

(*a*) Compare Green, *Political Obligation*, chap. 'Will, not force, is the basis of the State.

(*b*) Mill divided actions into self-regarding and other-regarding and conceded absolute liberty in the former sphere, though he was conscious of the fact that such clear-cut division is not strictly logical. See *On Liberty* ch. 4, 5. So also in Spencer, though he seems to modify it by his theories of evolution and the nature of social organism. Rousseau and Hobbes based their *Contrat*

Spencer constructed their theories of liberty and individualism with the help of this mode of thinking, and thus served to give precision and life to the concepts of liberty and rights.

It would not be improper therefore, if we begin our classification of law from the standpoint of *origin* in the sophistic way.

The origin of law is either human or non-human; *i. e.*, law is either original and not a handiwork of man, or law is a humanly-created institution. Law of non-human origin may be of three kinds. First of all, (no chronology is implied) there is the law which is directly created and promulgated by God. The Hebrew theory of law in which Moses is depicted as receiving law from Jehovah is an instance to the point. Hammurabi of ancient Egypt is also said to have received the laws from the sun-god Shamash, and there is said to be an engraving showing Hammurabi actually receiving the code. This is what is known as the theological conception of law.

Secondly, there is the conception that there exists an original law, but that human beings are required to find out that law by the exercise of some human faculty, designated variously as reason, intuition or that peculiar faculty of knowing truths possessed by those seers of thought, the Hindu rishis. Stoicism is an aspect of this metaphysical conception of law.

Social and *Leviathan* on this method of reasoning. So the clear-cut issues of Life and Non-life have receded into the background because of Jagadish Bose's researches into plant life. The fact is that there is a continuity in all phenomena.

Here there is no deity to promulgate the law(*a*), but the law of nature is found out by man with the help of his reason, which is only a partial manifestation of the Universal Reason pervading the entire nature. Stoical conception of law is more a conception of order, harmony, simplicity and universalism, than a conception of law as a rule of conduct(*b*), though order is nothing but the result of a rule of conduct. This metaphysical conception of law as morality, of rules of conduct which we ought to follow, is either rationalistic or intuitive, is either deduced by processes of reasoning or found out *a priori* by intuition. The value of this metaphysical conception of *natural law* lies, not in framing our laws on the pattern of the *laws of nature* (for that is absurd), but rather, in furnishing us with a notion, that there is an ideal and eternal standard of justice, to which we can appeal when we suffer injustice. Much harm has been done by the confusion of law of nature as setting a standard with laws of nature meaning statements of causal connection and generalisation ; and the two notions ought to be kept entirely distinct, for, an analysis of natural laws, however acute it might be, can never give us a standard. In other words, "ought" should not be confused with "is" (*c*).

(*a*) In some cases the word of the Deity is identified with the intuition and commands of the reason. For a short history of the theory of Law of Nature see Pulszky, *Theory of Law and Civil Society*.

(*b*) This is because there has been a confusion of natural law (ought) with the laws of nature (is), the latter signifying a certain order and harmony in the material universe.

(*c*) For diverse conceptions included under the cate-

The sophistry involved in making two things appear as antithetical, is apparent when we come to study the origin and nature of custom. Custom, specially in primitive times, was looked upon as uncreated, and hence followed with respect. Human society differs from an animal society in the fact, that over and above the phenomenon of physical aggregation, there is the consciousness, to a greater or lesser extent, of this aggregation; but custom has emerged as an objective rule of conduct, even before mankind has found itself grouped into what Prof. Giddings would call an Ethnogenic Association(*a*). It would not be wrong to say that custom exists as an objective fact even in Zoogenic and Anthropogenic Associations. When mankind is just beginning to live the lives of human beings, it already finds its conduct being guided by customs, of which the origin is lost in hoary antiquity. Again, similarity in conduct which gives rise to custom, is mostly to be explained by the two most primary psychological phenomena of impression and imitation. Now, this imitative tendency of mankind which lies at the root of customs(*b*) is mostly an impulse; the element of deliberation is absent, at least, in the primitive stages of society; and where a phenomenon has its origin in

gory Law of Nature, see the article 'Law of Nature' by Taylor in the *Annals of the American Academy of Pol. and Soc. Sciences*, April 1891. Taylor has concluded that the Law of Nature is relative.

(*a*) *Principles of Sociology.*

(*b*) Tarde, the French Sociologist, explains the phenomenon of Society by imitation, while Giddings puts forward the fact of consciousness of kind as the essential factor in the birth and evolution of society.

imitative instinct, we would naturally assign to it a non-human origin. It is because of this fact, that custom is looked upon as sacred or even God-given, and hence the conception of *law governing human society*, even if we reject the theological and metaphysical origins of law(*a*).

We now pass on to consider law as a phenomenon of human creation. By 'human creation' we mean, that rules of conduct have been instituted by human beings for the purpose of subserving certain ends. This perception of end is the essential feature which distinguishes the conception of law as of human origin from that of non-human origin. But really we cannot distinguish perception of end from non-perception of end; there is a gradual shading of the one into the other, there is no sudden break and consciousness of an end is a matter of slow growth. This will be evident from a further discussion about the nature of custom. In well-advanced societies, customs serve as rules of conduct, not because they are of non-human origin, but because they serve certain ends. The moment we begin to observe customs with this *consciousness* of their utility, that moment they acquire the character of human origin. The modern customs are of human origin, though it will be difficult, if not impossible, to assign them to any definite source. We view custom, not as something *uncreated* and original, as the primitive people did, but we look upon it as a *growth*, in which both instinctive imitation and

(*a*) All these conceptions will be seen in the various Hindu theories of law.

deliberate imitation, unconsciousness and consciousness have mingled.

There is a class of laws of human origin which can be assigned to definite sources(*a*). They are enacted by sovereign bodies, and are technically known as positive laws ; or they are imposed by non-sovereign societies and are recognised as rules of conduct by the members of those societies(*b*). These societies may be formed within one state, or they may be international societies.

Here is our scheme of classification :—

- LAW
  - Non-Human Origin
    - Theological (Moses, Shamash) (1)
    - Metaphysical (Law of Nature, Reason, Intuition) (2)
    - Custom (Uncreated, Sacred, Objective) (3)
  - Human Origin
    - Custom (Growth, Objective and Subjective Aspects) (4)
    - Rules of Non-Sovereign Societies (Trade-guilds, Village Community) (5)
    - Positive Laws (Austinian sense) (6)

(*a*) We are going to discuss whether these sources are historical and material or juridical and formal.

(*b*) Customs and rules of non-sovereign societies as such are called positive morality by Austin.

Possibly in this scheme of classification we have made ourselves liable to the charge of confusion between historical and juridical origins of law. Yet as a matter of fact, the above classification *fairly* represents the truth from both points of view (*i. e.* historical and juridical origins).

Firstlv, let us examine the classification from the standpoint of *material* source. In (1) the material sources of law are due to God, as when Moses is said to have got the laws from the Jewish god. In (2) reason or intution is said to discover the rules of law. In (3) the uncreated objective customs give us the rules of conduct. Similarly in (4); but in (5) and (6) the material sources may be had from (5) and (6) or from somewhere else (generally custom). Generally, but not in all cases(*a*), the materials for (5) and (6) are already there(*b*). Probably this is what Gierke means when he says that "law is the result of a common conviction not that a thing shall be, but that it is".

When we come to consider law from the standpoint of *juridic* origin, the question that confronts us is the question of *authority*. Of course in all these cases *a sanction of some kind* must indeed be implied, but this sanction is not always inflicted by a definite tribunal. With this qualification in view, we may say that the law given by a deity is obeyed because it represents the command of that deity and hence

(*a*) When this is the case, the law often remains a dead-letter, *e. g.* Juvenile Smoking Act in Bengal.

(*b*) Compare the mechanical and organic views of law.

theological law is a sort of divine positive law. The authority of law implied in (2) is also in the nature of an Imperative, but it is a self-imposed command. The difference between (1) and (2) is the difference between "must" and "ought". In (3), the driving force is mainly instinct, and the authority is the mere fact that all behave in like manner; but perhaps even here, there is the vague fear of supernatural being and public opinion, or the conviction that non-observance is not desirable(*a*). In (4), (5) and (6) the fundamental feature is express or tacit agreement or recognition, and this provides the requisite authority. None the less, the psychology of average men in observing rules of conduct is highly complex: it is a mixture of imitative instinct, fear and duty in variable proportions(*b*).

With these remarks we may pass on to the interpretation of Hindu theories of law.

The first problem to which we are to address ourselves, is whether the Vedic Aryans had any conception of law, and if they had, then what was the nature of their jural conceptions. Henceforth we would frequently use the technical Hindu word *dharma* signifying law(*c*).

(*a*) See Mackenzie, *Manual of Ethics*, pp. 256-7.

(*b*) An average Bengali Hindu does not drink for 3 reasons:—(1) His fellow countrymen do not drink. (2) He is afraid of public opinion. (3) He considers drinking to be immoral.

(*c*) The term Dharma is also used in the senses of justice, duty, virtue and religion of which the last two are categories of ethics and theology. Benoy Kumar Sarkar has differentiated these five senses (*Pol. Institutions and Theories of the Hindus*, p. 206) but he should have added

Even in the Rig-Veda, the term dharma occurs, as where Varuna is referred to as the upholder of dharma(*a*). There are other occasions when this word has been used(*b*), mainly in connection with religious rites and ceremonies. Now what did the Aryans mean by this dharma? Certainly, even in the Rig-Vedic age, dharma meant some rules of conduct, but they referred to *binding habits*, 'determined by the inner-nature of the group man and according to the action upon it of the forces and necessities of his environment'. The rules as yet were not imposed by self-conscious group-mind, because the social aggregate was only possessed of a mechanical mentality of which imitation was the most important constituent. Now these binding habits* were there as objective facts even before the Vedic Hindus were conscious of their existence, and it was their imitative instinct which

that the term dharma as a category of Jurisprudence (law) has got a peculiar meaning to the Sutra- and Smriti-writers at least. The law of causality was laid under contribution in setting forth the dharma rules of conduct. Some actions of men, so it is assumed, have got consequences even when men are dead. This consequence is known as *apurva*—a property which inheres in the soul. If the deeds of a man are virtuous, then through the agency of this *apurva* force the man will enjoy in the life to come eternal bliss; if not, the very opposite will happen. The significance of this philosophy of life had a great influence on Hindu theories of punishment. The term dharma was used for those rules of conduct the observance of which would lead to dharma, i.e. eternal bliss through the agency of *apurva* force in the soul.

(*a*) Varuna is rather the keeper of the law than its creator. In one or two places ordinances are said to be Varuna's, but then they refer to 'natural' *rita*.

(*b*) Rv. III, 3, 1; V, 63, 7. Av. XI, 7, 17; XII, 5, 7. (All these Vedic references are quoted from *Vedic Index* Part I by Macdonell and Keith)

really explained their adherence to dharma or law and custom. The Vedic Hindus were simply surprised at this upholding of custom, and their peculiar psychology, so full of deities, was immediately laid under contribution, and the result was, that one of the gods *e. g.* Varuna was conceived of as upholder of custom. Where we moderners would say that imitative instinct was the upholder of the law in that stage of civilisation, the Vedic Hindus would say that it is Varuna who is really *dharmapati.*

The conception of dharma or law as something created by someone, does not seem to be familiar to the Vedic Hindus, though in the Upanishadic age we happen to come across a conception of law as a creation(*a*). Varuna is the dharmapati, the upholder or protector of the law and not the creator(*b*). We have seen that even in Zoogenic Association there is something akin to rules of conduct; it is clear therefore, that the Vedic Hindus were confronted with objective customs before they were even conscious of the fact. They probably did not enquire about their origin, but took them for granted as natural. To them the problem at first appeared as to who would protect the dharma or customary law, and they seem to have solved it by giving this task to Varuna.

That the Vedic Hindus had some conception of law as a standard of conduct is also evident from the

(*a*) This will be explained shortly.

(*b*) The Teutonic theory views law not as a creation, but as something which exists as a part of the tribal life. Cf. the organic theory of law.

fact that they looked upon adultery, seduction and sorcery with disapproval(*a*).

There is another conception in the Vedas which is intimately connected with the concept dharma. This is *rita*, meaning the order and harmony in the universe. Varuna is also the upholder of order in the universe and in human society, and hence his surname is *ritasya gopa*, meaning the gopa or guardian of *rita* or order(*b*). Varuna is both *dharmapati* and *ritasya gopa* and rightly so ; for the twin conceptions of law and order, dharma and rita are intimately connected. These two conceptions are logically related to each other as cause and effect: rita being the effect of dharma, the cause. But if these two conceptions are applied to natural phenomena, dharma and rita tend to merge into each other, for law in the scientific sense of sequence and co-existence is another name for order and harmony(*c*).

Now if it be admitted that there existed rules of conduct, and imitative instinct, or in Vedic phraseology, a particular deity, upheld those rules, still there might be actual violations of those customs. It is probable that the wronged man was tacitly empowered to do what he liked and in cases of murder the principle of an eye for an eye was followed. The

(*a*) Barth, *Religions of India*, pp. 32-4. The vice of gambling is also hinted at in the cursing hymn of Vasistha ; see Ragozin, *Vedic India*, pp. 377-8.
(*b*) *Ibid*, p. 17.
(*c*) The Stoics identified the law of reason with laws of nature (in the scientific sense). The one is concerned with laying down rules of conduct, while the other refers to statement of causal connection. It is a confusion between 'ought' and 'is'.

Vedic kings at first could not take cognizance of these crimes because they were so very busy with their military duties. The principle of unregulated revenge cannot long exist without impairing the stability of the society, and sooner or later the Vedic kings found that this anarchy within the society considerably interfered with their military duties. Hence the Vedic king was compelled, when he felt himself powerful enough, to regulate this private revenge and enforce the system of wergeld(*a*).

The assumption of judicial jurisdiction by the king or the tribal chief is certainly a thing of later growth and it is the criminal jurisdiction which is first taken in hand. Before his assumption of this jurisdiction there were other persons(*b*) who exercised this jurisdiction, though not in a systematic manner. Our point is that before the tribal chief has assumed judicial jurisdiction custom has developed. This conclusion challenges directly the contention of Maine that "however strongly we, with our modern associations, may be inclined to lay down *a priori* that the notion of a custom must precede that of a judicial sentence, and that a judgment must affirm a custom or punish its breach, it seems quite certain that the historical order of the ideas is that in which I have placed them" (*viz.*, judicial sentence and then custom)(*c*).

(*a*) *Vedic Index* I, pp. 391-2.

(*b*) *Madhyamasi* stands for arbiter.

(*c*) *Ancient Law* ch. I. Maine's dictum that judicial sentence historically precedes a custom is not, in our opinion, tenable on the following grounds. (a) Custom,

In the early Vedic age we have got the conceptions of dharma and rita, but it is a deity and not the tribal chief who is the protector of dharma and guardian of rita. As yet there seems to be no acute dualism between god and man or nature and man, for Varuna is the upholder of order in the universe and in human society. Before the assumption of judicial jurisdiction by the tribal chief, customary modes of action have grown up ; some of which because of natural selection tend to be preserved while others go to the wall. The residuary customs serve as standards of conduct because they have got social value. In other words, biological forces in the beginning determine the nature of customary morality (if it can be called morality at all, because it means instinctive adherence to those customs which have been selected by nature)(*a*). The sanction for the observance of customs in an age where no tribal chief but a deity is the upholder thereof, lay in the feeling of vague uneasiness conse-

already from the very birth of human society, exists as an objective fact, and this must have struck primitive imagination. This resulted in the enunciation of the well-known theory that law is uncreated. Therefore Maine's quotation from Grote (*History of Greece*) that the human king is not a law-maker but a judge is pointless. (b) The judicial function of a king is a thing of later growth. Before that private arbitration came and it cannot be said that Themis dictated Themistes to these ordinary *madhyamasis*. (c)The conception of order in the universe may inspire a notion of custom in the human mind, for as we have seen before, *dharma* or law and *rita* or order are intimately related. (d) Savages have also their notions of customs. The fact is that the notion is instinctive. Maine finds the germ of custom in similarity of awards, whereas we think that custom has grown out of imitative instinct.

(*a*) Probably this is the case in connection with adultery, sorcery etc. referred to before.

quent on the violation of a settled habit of action and this feeling is likely to be intensified when coupled with the fact that Varuna, the tribal god, the dharmapati, (the conception of a tribal god also intensifies the conception of social unity)(*a*) may not like it.

Unlike the Sophists, to the Rig-Vedic Hindus there was no dualism between nature and man. The conception of rita or order was transplanted from the material to the spiritual world or rather there was one rita for both nature and man, and the enforcer of this rita in all cases was Varuna. Therefore when man was guilty of violating any social custom—and this custom was the manifestation of rita in the human sphere—it was Varuna, who, as the *gopa* of *rita* in the material and human worlds, inflicted punishment. And this punishment was of various kinds. Varuna might deliver the rita-breaker unto death or "to the blow of the furious" or "to the wrath of the spiteful" and in his anger might trouble the wrong-doer with disease. In all this there is a decided advance in thought, because here unlike the savage tribes, the Dayaks and the Battas (quoted before), the wrong-doer is conscious of his individual wrong. The conception of moral wrong is beginning to emerge, though it is still clouded by the fact that it is disease or death inflicted by Varuna which prevents one from

(*a*) Social unity suffers if there are many gods. But even in the Vedic age a struggle for existence was going on among the different gods and Varuna is generally successful in this struggle. Indra is often a very important god. See hymn IV, 42. (Quoted in Ragozin, *Vedic India*, p. 203).

breaking the custom or rita. In short, the hymns of repentance that Vasistha offers to Varuna, point us to the conclusion that the sanction was supplied by the anger of Varuna directly manifesting itself in darkness (of which all primitive men are mightily afraid) disease and death and similar punishments.

In the age when Satapatha Brahman was composed the conception of law has changed a bit and possibly this is a case of theory adjusting itself to actual facts(*a*). The tribal chief is at first a war-leader. In the fight between Devas and Asuras the Devas were defeated and they attributed their defeat to the fact that they had no kings to lead them in war. So they consented to elect a king to fight the Asuras(*b*). Apart from the fact that this implies an elective origin of kingship among the Devas (*i. e.* the Aryas), what is important from our standpoint is the fact that he is only a war-leader. But it is natural that a war-leader cannot successfully conduct war unless he can maintain order within his jurisdiction. Hence the war-leader becomes also the executive ruler, but executive rulership in order to be real, must also include judicial administration(*c*), specially on the criminal side.

(*a*) This relativity of theory to institutions can be seen in the Stoical theory of law universal and the break-up of City-States ; in 15th and 16th century European States and Renaissance Sovereignty and in the rise of modern group-organisation and Laski's conception of sovereignty, and also in the history of Northern India before the rise of the Mauryas and the Kautilyan conception of *Mandala*.

(*b*) *Aitareya Brahman* I, 14.

(*c*) This is how we can justify the *droit administratif* of France.

Now this was the state of society which was responsible for this changed conception of dharma. In the Satapatha Brahman in connection with the description of the Rajasuya rites the following passage occurs:—"For Varuna Dharmapati (the Lord of the Law) he then prepares a Varuna pap of barley; thereby Varuna, the Lord of the Law, makes him Lord of the Law; and that truly is the supreme State, when one is Lord of the Law; for whoever attains to the supreme State, to him they come in (matters of) Law: therefore to Varuna Dharmapati(*a*)". We have passed the stage when sanction for custom lay in Varuna the dharmapati and have come to a stage when the king is the dharmapati, the protector of the law. Protection of law, we have seen, along with its concomitant, the judicial administration, has just been taken over by the war-leader. Thus when the war-leader has assumed executive and judicial administration of the law, the former theory of Varuna as dharmapati was replaced by the theory of king as dharmapati. But the transition was gradual, because even in the above quotation, it is Varuna who makes the king the lord of the law. The conception of law as uncreated still reigns supreme: it is still the customary epoch; only the protector or rather the enforcer of law has changed and even this change is not abrupt. In the above quotation, the two functions, *viz.* executive rulership (internal) and adjudication, are referred to.

Jayaswal is of opinion that "the old theory had

(*a*) *Sat. Brah.* V, 3, 3, 9 (S.B.E. Vol. 41).

been that the law of the community was administered by the community(*a*). His theory is likely to hold good if the Sabha of old really performed some judicial functions like the Greek Apella, but his interpretations, while he is trying to put forward the proposition that "the Sabha acted as the national judicature," are really far-fetched(*b*).

Thus by wielding the danda(*c*), the king is upholding the dharma. Of course dharma was in existence before the appearance of the king's danda (when the king was a mere war-leader), but with the growing complexities of the society and possibly because of moral depravity dharma cannot exist without the king's danda(*d*). Of course dharma as law is uncreated(*e*), but the king's danda gives dharma a concrete shape. When the king has been made dharmapati and when his danda has been so much

(*a*) *Hindu Polity*, part II, p. 23.

(*b*) *Ibid*, part I, pp. 18-20. See also part II, p. 160. As to the divergent opinions held about the nature and functions of the Sabha by Ludwig, Zimmer and Hillebrandt see Narendra Law's *Aspects of Ancient Indian Polity* pp. 24-27 and also Pramathanath Banerjee's *Public Administration in Ancient India*, p. 95 footnote. See *Vedic Index* under Sabha and Samiti.

(*c*) Danda means executive power or the power of sovereignty. It is one of the fundamental concepts in Hindu political thought. For a vivid picture of danda see *Santiparva* (R.P.) sec. 121.

(*d*) Kamandaka, *Nitiṣara* II, 40-2 ; *Sukraniti* IV-I, lines 92 and following ; *Manu* VII, 14, 15, 18, *Santiparva* (R. P.) sec. 69, sl. 20.

(*e*) Benoy Kumar Sarkar writes, 'Dharma (law) is the creation of the State (*Political Institutions*, p. 207). He ought to have put some adjective (e.g. objective) before the word creation.'

idealized, it is possible that the people or the king may take danda to be superior to dharma. To provide against such a contingency, the king is required to go through a highly significant ceremony. "The king comes back immediately to the throne which he again ascends while the priest recites ; 'Sit thee on the pleasant soft-seated throne'. Then follows an exceedingly queer procedure. The king's person is silently touched on the back with a rod which is the symbolic sceptre of justice, conveying by the action the view of the sacred common law that the king was not above but under the law. The interpretation given of this procedure is an amusing piece of euphemism. The commentator says that it is done to carry the king's person beyond 'judicial destruction' (danda-vadha)(*a*)". The commentator's explanation that henceforth the king becomes exempt from punishment (adandya) is incompatible with the theory of law as uncreated. Had law been viewed as something created by the fiat of the king, then of course the king's exemption from punishment becomes intelligible ; but as it is, the ceremony means not only that the king is under the law(*b*), as Jayaswal explains, but also that this danda will smite the king (mark the symbolism in the ceremony) if he does not handle this danda righteously(*c*). In fact, subsequent writers

(*a*) The whole quotation is from Jayaswal's *Hindu Polity* part II, p. 35 and his interpretation of the significance of the ceremony is correct. The ceremony is described in *Satapatha-Brahman* V, 4, 4, 7 (S.B.E. Vol. 41).

(*b*) In *Manu* kings are fined.

(*c*) This danda is a double-edged dagger. See *Manu* VII, 27-28.

have all emphasized this aspect of danda and they have raised it to the status of an abstract principle of force.

Up to this time the theory is that the law or dharma is uncreated and the king only enforces it. When customs are few and social life is simple, we meet with no difficulty in knowing the contents of law, even if the theory of law as uncreated be accepted. But with the growing complexities of society caused by the differentiation of castes(*a*) of which we get an inkling in the *Sat. Brah.* and the evolution of which perhaps began in the later Rig-Vedic age(*b*), it becomes increasingly difficult to know the law. This is one of the turning points in the history of the evolution of law. The Brahmins are beginning to assert their supremacy in the society and they are frequently coming into collision with the king representing the Khattriya caste(*c*). Another aspect of this friction is represented by the Jaina and Buddhis-

(*a*) In the *Sat. Brah.* we find references to the evolution of four castes thus indicating the complex nature of the society. The mutual relation of the Brahmins and the Khattriyas, originally the two important castes, are also referred to.

(*b*) *Purusa-sukta,*—for a brief history about castes and classes in the Rig-Vedic age, see ch. II, *Indo-Aryan Polity* by Prafulla Basu. See Ragozin, *Vedic India*, pp. 280-1.

(*c*) The story of Parasuram. The story of the rishis killing Vena proves this (See *Santiparva* sec. 59, sl. 93-4, 106-11). Jayaswal's interpretation of this story as 'Brahmanisation of the theory' and 'overstatement of Brahman claim" due to Pushyamitra having ascended the throne, does not, I am afraid, go to the root of the matter. See *Hindu Polity*, part II, pp. 47-8 footnote.

tic(*a*) revolts (led by Khattriya princes) against a Brahmin-ridden social system. The post-Vedic king with his danda has actually become very powerful, and he was the only upholder of dharma and as such he was the only man as yet credited with a knowledge of the dharma. But the growing power of the priestly oligarchy(*b*) wanted to monopolise the knowledge of the laws, and hence sought to introduce several important attributes in the concept "dharma."

The first proposition put forward was that the Brahmins were also the upholders of the dharma in conjunction with the king. But this did not advance the cause of the Brahmins very much, for as yet in theory, the law was uncreated and surely the king with his danda was the real upholder of, and in a sense the creator of, dharma. The problem that confronted the sacerdotal caste still remained unsolved. The Brahmins would not remain satisfied by being merely the upholders of the law,—and it is worse than useless without the danda, which was the monopoly of the king,—they also wanted to give the law a sacred character which would be in keeping with their sacerdotal caste and sacred functions. A theory was formulated that law was of theological origin, that it was derived from the will of the creator. But what if the king laid claim to the sole knowledge of

(*a*) The contempt of Buddha for the Brahmins is well-illustrated in a dialogue between Vasettha and Gotama. See *Evolution of Indian Polity* by Shamasastri p. 105.

(*b*) In Greece and Rome there were similar priestly oligarchies.

law direct from the creator. That path was blocked by the formulation of the theory of cosmic creation. The original creative principle created the Khattriyas and the other inferior castes, but the Brahmin was the direct manifestation of the creative principle. Now let us realise the implications of these propositions.

We have seen that the Brahmins claimed to be upholders of law along with the king(*a*), and have noted the fact that by itself it means nothing. Then the theory of theological origin of law was formulated in the *Brihadaranyaka Upanishad.* It runs thus: "He (God) was not strong enough. He created still further the most excellent dharma (law). Law is the Ksattra of the Ksattra, therefore there is nothing higher than Law(*b*)". This theory of law as created by the will of the creator, coupled with the theory of the origin of castes just referred to, is highly interesting from our standpoint. The king as before is placed under the law, for law is the Khattra of the Khattra, and law is derived from the will of the creator, but Brahmin is the direct manifestation of the creator, and therefore it follows that the will of the Brahmin, the creative principle incarnate on the earth, is the law. It also follows that law is sacred in a more intensive sense.

The law which now boasts of a theological origin, is not of the same nature as the Mosaic Decalogue, though the latter has got a theological origin. The

(*a*) *Sat. Brah.* V, 4,4,5 (S.B.E. Vol. 41).
(*b*) *Brih. Up.* I,4,14 (S.B.E. Vol. I5).

Jewish law is of divine origin in this respect that Moses got it wholesale from Jehovah. Nor can we compare it with the new customs of Mahomed, dictated(*a*) to the prophet by Allah, while the former happened to be in states of mind which we call *samadhi*. With a certain end in view, the author of the Brihadaranyaka merely formulated the theory of the origin of law: it was an empty theory without any contents. As we shall see just now, the theory was rather metaphysical than theological.

The metaphysical aspect of law is seen in the Brihadaranyaka Upanishad from which we have just quoted. After declaring that law is created by God, the author proceeds: "Thus the law is what is called the true. And if a man declares what is true, they say he declares the law; and if he declares the law, they say he declares what is true. Thus both are the same(*b*)." This metaphysical aspect is also hinted at when we find the following passage in the Sat. Brah.: "The first libation of ghee is the sacred law, and the second the truth; and verily he secures for himself law and truth, and whatsoever is to be gained by law and truth, all that he now gains(*c*)." In another passage, the king, though the upholder of the law, is asked to speak and do what is right.

The significance of the quotation from the Brihadaranyaka lies in the fact that in the very same passage law is described as the *creation of God*

(*a*) Compare the Delphic Oracle.

(*b*) S.B.E. Vol. 15.

(*c*) S.B.E. Vol. 44.

and also equivalent to a declaration of what is *true*. This is viewing law as having both a theological and a metaphysical origin. But this is not contradictory as it seems at first. Hinduism as depicted in the Upanishads knows no prophet like Moses or Mahomed. Hence the difference in theological origin between the Hindu view on one side and the Hebraic conception on the other. But the rishis of the Upanishads are seers of truth; therefore the truths which they come to know by intuitive processes are identical with the commands of the creator. Hence there is no inherent contradiction between these two conceptions of the origin of law, *viz.* theological and metaphysical. Another point to be noted in this connection is that the Upanishadic age generally represents a period of metaphysical thinking (though Philosophy began even in the Rig-Veda, e.g. the famous cosmogonic hymn beginning with "nor aught nor naught existed then").

A parallel(*a*) to this Hindu conception can be found in a speech of Demosthenes against Aristogeiton. The latter is charged by the former as a typical law-breaker, and in a speech the former unfolds the nature of the law. It is said that "the law is sacred in its origin being a gift of the Gods; that it is instituted by wise men(*b*)". The former portion of this quotation stands for theological origin in theory only, while the metaphysical aspect is supplied by

(*a*) See Vinogradoff, *Historical Jurisprudence*, Vol. II p. 18.

(*b*) Of course there are some other points in Demosthenes' speech which have no parallel in our quotation.

the "wise men", the rishis. The Stoic conception is similar, though not identical. We have seen that the Stoics confused between law in the scientific sense and law in the ethical or legal sense. Still the Stoic conception of law of reason has its parallel in our quotation, the only difference being that the Stoics depended on reason and logic for discovering law, while our rishis depended on "intuition" (*a*). Aristotle also conceived law as the rule of reason and hence of God.

The concept of law as depicted in the Upanishad from which we have quoted, implies that dharma is the will of the creator and also is equivalent to truth. It is a fine combination of objectivism and subjectivism. It is not correct to equate law and morality (*b*) on the strength of this quotation, nor is it true to say that this represents an ethical conception of law (*c*). All that is implied is simply that truth is law and law is truth. Here we are concerned with the ideal of truth and not directly with the ideal of good. It is better therefore to view it as a metaphysical conception of law rather than as an ethical one.

A conception of law whose origin is either divine or is to be found in the common reason of mankind or again where it is discovered by the peculiar "intuitive" faculty of our rishis and equated with truth

(*a*) Cicero's ethical teaching based on Stoic principles is intuitionist. He appeals to conscience. See Ritchie, *Natural Rights* pp. 35-36. Cicero's intuitionism is rather tinged with emotion and equity (Pulszky, *Theory of Law and Civil Society*).

(*b*) Ghoshal, *Hindu Political Theories* p. 55.

(*c*) Benoy Sarkar, *Political Institutions* etc. p. 208.

cannot *a priori* but be regarded as universal and immutable. Whether the Hindus had any such conception or not will be clear as we proceed.

At this stage (when we are entering the Sutra period) it would be better to sharply differentiate *sacred law* from *non-sacred law*. Strictly speaking, sacred law regulates only those actions of the Aryans which would lead to the *apurva* quality of the soul. Thus there is a two-fold qualification attached to the term "sacred". On the one hand, it excludes the non-Aryans as such from the dominion of sacred law(*a*), and on the other, all sorts of conduct of the Aryans are not sought to be regulated by the sacred law. Theoretically the province of law may be divided thus :—

LAW (dharma in a wider sense)

- For Aryans (A)
  - Sacred Law (*dharma, narrower sense*) (C) (Different for different Castes and Orders)
  - (D) Secular Law
- For non-Aryans (B) (no distinction as between (C) & (D)

Much harm has been done by failing to distinguish between these departments of law. The scope of the Dharmasutras and the Dharmasastras generally(*b*) is confined to (C). This (C) department

(*a*) The Romans at first excluded the barbarians from the pale of Civil Law. *Jus Gentium* was the result of this policy of exclusion.

(*b*) Manu in his work (I, 118) often deals with (B) and (D). Compare Baudhayan I, 1, 2 (S. B. E. Vol. 14) and

of law comprises duties for the various varnas and asrams.

Now we are in a position to answer the query as to whether law is universal and immutable. The idea of law (whether of theological or metaphysical origin) being held in equal authority without reference to any particular class is discredited by the Sutra- and Smriti-writers who would formulate sacred law only for the Aryans. Then again within sacred law itself the idea of universality is absent because of the caste-system. The idea of immutability holds good, in theory at least, in the cases of laws for different castes, though in abnormal times the doctrine of swadharma is held in abeyance; but this idea is entirely absent in (B) and (D)(*a*). The fact is that the conception of law as found in the Brihadaranyaka is merely a metaphysical one. It is a fit conception for a forest-treatise without any realistic setting. The Stoic conception of law had a brilliant history(*b*),

Vasistha XIX, 7 (S. B. E. Vol. 14). Gautama XI, 20-21 (S. B. E. Vol. II). The *sreni*, *puga*, *gana*, *samgha dharma* etc., referred to by Manu, Yagnabalka and others illustrate (B) and (D) departments of law or dharma in the wider sense. See Ramesh Chandra Majumdar's *Corporate Life in Ancient India.*

(*a*) For a contrary view see Radhakamal Mukerjee's *Democracies in the East*, p. 127. The author has not distinguished the different departments of law and hence his error. Nevertheless he modifies his principles of universality and immutability by the opposite principle of relativity.

(*b*) The Stoic conception wielded tremendous influence over Roman Law, French Law, Grotian system of International Law and Rousseau's Politics culminating in French Rsvolution. See Maine, *Ancient Law* ch. IV and Bryce, *Studies in History and Jurisprudence* Vol. II pp. 120-171.

but this Hindu metaphysical conception wielded effective influence in the province of sacred law only.

Now let us pass on to the study of dharma *par excellence*, the subject matter of the Dharmasutras. All the Dharmasutras presuppose a divinely-ordained social structure known as varnasram(*a*), governed in many matters by the eternal law or dharma (in the restricted sense). But these twin concepts of dharma and varnasram, so closely related to each other that we cannot conceive of the one without the other, are mere empty concepts, so long as the danda of the king does not help them to manifest themselves in this world of senses.

All the authors of the Dharmasutras pay lip-homages to Veda as the real source of sacred law. To the Hindus the Veda stands for the word of God, it is the eternal embodiment of truth. But in reality the Vedic origin is of a juridical nature. Here we should be on our guard against confusing historical or material with formal or juridical origin. When the authors of the Dharmasutras refer to Veda as the sole source of law, they mean formal source. Ultimately, no doubt, the formal source is to be traced to the Being who willed the law, but proximately the juridical authority is the Veda.

When Apastamba(*b*) says : "And (the authority for the latter) the Vedas alone", he means juridical source. Again the same thing is implied by Gautama(*c*),

(*a*) The *Chandogya Upanishad* (II, 23, 1 and 2 ; S. B. E. Vol. 1) recounts three branches of asram law.

(*b*) I. 1, 1, 3 (S. B. E. Vol. II).

(*c*) I, 1 (S. B. E. Vol. II).

when he lays down that "the Veda is the source of the sacred law". Vasistha's(*a*) authority for sacred law is also juridical when he says that "the sacred law has been settled by the revealed texts". Similar is the case wih Baudhayan(*b*).

But the material sources of the sacred law are to be found in the traditions(*c*) and practices(*d*) of men learned in the Vedas and also in the decisions(*e*) of a body of learned men formed to settle the law. The traditions of the learned and the practices of the *sistas* are only authoritative, because they are supposed to the based on the Veda. Just as Austin would not call any and every rule of conduct a positive law, unless it derives its authority from the legal sovereign—the juridical source of law, so the practices of the sistas and the traditions of the learned would not be included in the category of sacred law unless they get their formal imprimatur from the Veda. But the Vedas are not the material sources as well, so how to know whether the traditions and practices are in accordance with the Veda. The theory says that the rules of conduct laid down or followed by men, "who have been properly obedient (to their teachers), who are aged, of subdued senses, neither given to avarice, nor hypocrites", or who are free

(*a*) I, 4 (S. B. E. Vol. 14).

(*b*) I, 1, 1, 1 (S. B. E. Vol. 14). Pramathanath Banerjee has failed to distinguish the formal from the material sources. See *Pub. Adm. in Ancient India* pp. 132-4.

(*c*) Gaut. I, 2 ; Vasistha I, 4 ; Baud, I, 1, 1, 3.

(*d*) Gaut. I, 2 ; Vasistha I, 5 ; Baud, I, 1, 1, 4.

(*e*) Apas. I, 1, 1, 1 ; Gaut. XVIII, 48 ; Vasistha III, 7 ; Baud. I, 1, 1, 7.

from pride, envy, arrogance, anger, know the Vedas and also how to draw inferences, are sacred laws. Here we have got a parallel case. As the metaphysical conception of the law of nature acquired a local habitation and name when Cicero sought to equate it with the rules of conduct deduced by the conscience of men not yet morally depraved, so the barren source of the Veda was fertilized by the authors of the Dharmasutras, when they in their turn laid down that the traditions and rules of conduct followed by the sistas or sages were *ipso facto* the *vidhis* of the Vedas. Just as the lost code of nature was supposed to have been found in Jus Gentium, so we might say that the lost vidhis of the Vedas (really they were not lost: they never existed) were re-incarnate in the *silas* (practices) of the sistas. From the metaphysical conception of law as truth (Brih. Up.) we have come to the ethical conception of law as morality. The ideal of truth has at last given birth to the ideal of goodness in conduct.

It is all right so far as the theory goes. But what would happen if the recollections of the sages be faint and if the practices and recollections of these men differ from one another, as is extremely natural. It was a dangerous principle which the authors of the Dharmasutras enunciated when they bestowed this authority of declaring the sacred law (*i.e.*, the practices of the sages formed the material sources of sacred law) upon any and every Brahmin who was a sista(*a*). Any emphasis on individual reason,

(*a*) For the definition of sista see Baud. I, 1, 1, 5-6.

or for the matter of that, individual "intuition", is bound to put a premium on anarchy in realms of thought and action. Law as the result of eternal will implies at the same time a conception of order and unity, but when individual reason attempts to find out the eternal rules of sacred law, the result will surely be all chaos and confusion, unless there is something else to hold in check the atomistic tendencies of individual reason.

Now the question is, what is this 'something else' which will bring order out of chaos and unity out of diversity. The solution lay in the Hindu institution of *Parishad*. These Parishads(*a*) were assemblies of three, five or ten men versed in the Veda, who were constituted to settle what is sacred law and what is not. Gautama, Vasistha and Baudhayan, all speak of Parishad, and Apastamba means the same thing when he says that 'the authority (for these duties) is the agreement of those who know the law'. Thus we come back to the intensely modern conception of law being founded on agreement and recognition. The sacred law was agreed to by the sages of the Parishad and recognised as such by the people, and the danda of the king was there to enforce it, so far as the king's danda can enforce it. The Parishad was, so to say, the hyphen that joined and co-ordinated the material and the juridical sources of sacred law.

The conception of sacred law as founded on agreement is one of the many peculiarities of the

(*a*) For a short account of these Parishads, see Naresh Sen Gupta's *Sources of Law and Society in Ancient India*, pp. 44-48.

pluralistic or multicellular polity of the Hindus. This pluralism in Hindu polity, so long as this pluralism was real, was mainly responsible for the absence of any mechanical conception of law as a fiat imposed by the king. (Exceptions will be noted later on)

In Greece, "in regard to sacral institutions and in all cases where religion was concerned, the influence of traditional usage asserted itself emphatically." And this traditional usage was authoritatively interpreted for popular benefit by professional representatives of legal lore, of which inscriptions record three classes. Of these one was a consultative board for matters connected with Eleusinian Mysteries. Mention is also made in Greece of a college of magistrates who declared or stated the law to the people(*a*). Again, the theory of law being founded on agreement as enunciated by Apastamba has its counterpart in that of Demosthenes, when the latter in his speech(*b*) against Aristogeiton says that law is sacred in its origin, being a gift of the gods; that it is instituted by wise men; * * * * and finally that it is a compact entered into by the members of the City(*c*).

The concept of law as developed in the Dharmasutras also implies the connected concept of justice.

(*a*) Vinogradoff, *Historical Jurisprudence* Vol. II, pp. 74-76.
(*b*) Ibid. p. 18.
(*c*) Here the conception of agreement is posited of a monistic State. But it should be remembered that the Greek monistic State is a City-State and not a Country-State.

The doctrine of varnasram or the division of the people into castes and orders represents a conception of social justice—eternally ordained no doubt—but organized by the danda of the king. The sacred law in fixing the duties of the various classes and asking each individual to fulfil his swadharma is only attacking the problem of justice from the standpoint of what is known to us as distributive justice. Considering the fact that the concept varnasram must have preceded the Sutra works which were composed in about 5th or 6th century B. C. (Jolly quoted in Majumdar's Intro. to 'Corporate Life'), we may be permitted to question the originality of the identical Platonic(*a*) conception of distributive justice. The conception of corrective justice has its Hindu analogue in penances, in the apurva theory and in the administration of sacred law by the king with the help of learned Brahmin judges. The State of the Sutra-period was thus the organizer of distributive and the administrator of corrective justice(*b*).

The *theory* of Parishad and the *fact* of pluralism point to the conclusion, that in the Sutra-period the fundamental background on which sacred law rested, was agreement; nevertheless, various kinds of sanctions(*c*) were attached to the rules of sacred law.

(*a*) The three elements according to Plato are the appetitive, spirited and rational, corresponding roughly to our Vaisya, Khattriya and Brahmin.

(*b*) See Muirhead and Hetherington, *Social Purpose*, p, 230.

(*c*) This subject requires separate treatment. Here a bare outline is given.

Ultimately, sacred law is the will of God, and hence a certain sanction attaches to the sacred law. This may be called the theological sanction. Again, the theory of *apurva*, which lies at the root of dharma *par excellence*, supplies the second kind of sanction. This sanction, so to say, is inherent in the action itself and is automatic, and is connected with the doctrine of *karma*. Since it is intimately related to metaphysical theories, it is better to designate it as metaphysical sanction. Finally, there is the sanction of the king's danda, even in cases of sacred law. This we may call as the positive sanction. What Bentham(*a*) calls political sanction has its prototype in the king's danda; his religious sanction is equivalent to our theological and metaphysical sanctions, and his moral sanction has its conterpart in Apastamba, when the latter, a pronounced believer in the relativity of virtue and sin, lays down in a remarkable passage, that "virtue and sin do not go about and say, 'Here we are', nor do gods, Gandharvas or Manes say (to men), 'This is virtue, this is sin'. But that is virtue, the practice of which wise men of the three twice-born castes praise; what they blame is sin(*b*)". What we have termed metaphysical sanction will

(*a*) Bentham, *Principles of Morals and Legislation*, ch. III.

(*b*) I. 7. 20, 6-7. Sukra has got a parallel passage (*Sacred Books of the Hindus*, Vol. XIII, V, 70-72) where he says that 'sins become virtues by a change of circumstances. That is virtue which is applauded by the many, that is vice which is cried down by all'. Public opinion as the standard, according to Sukra, is the opinion of "compact majority", as opposed to that of the 'cultured minority' of Apastamba. These are rudiments of evolutionary ethics no doubt.

16

probably be characterised by Mill(a) as a kind of external sanction; but still the germ of what Mill calls the internal sanction of conscience may be found in our metaphysical sanction. The complex apparatus of human motives is nowhere better illustrated than when we come to examine the nature of sanctions.

We have so far directed our attention to the concept of sacred law; but in the preceding classification it has been shown that sacred law by itself does not exhaust the whole province of law. There are two other provinces of law which we have designated as (B) and (D) departments of law. Of the two, the former is concerned with the customs of the non-Aryans, while (D) represents those rules of social conduct (for the Aryans) which do not properly fall within the scope of the Dharmasutras. From the standpoint of legal theory these two departments seem to be identical.

Custom was the material source of this law and agreement or recognition was, so to say, the juridical source. The Sutra period clearly gives us to understand that the Aryan polity visualized by the Sutra-writers was not monistic : in fact, every individual, because of his many-sidedness, was bound to come into relation with several groups. Thus, as a money-lender, he may be a member of an economic corporation; as a man interested in observing rules of marriage and diet, he is a member of a social corporation *viz.* caste, and again, as a villager, is a member of a small territorial corporation like the

(a) Mill, *Utilitarianism*, ch. III.

village community. Unlike the idealized Greek City-State, which penetrated every citizen in all his interests, the Hindu Country-State was pluralistic, and hence almost all the social relations of the individuals were absorbed by these corporations(*a*). The Hindu polity in the Sutra period was rather an association of individuals, already united in diverse groups, each with its own common life, in a more comprehensive group with the king at the head of the co-ordinating group. The monistic conception of the Greek State was realistic, because it was a City-State; and the pluralistic conception of the Hindu State was also realistic, because it was a Country-State.

It is therefore evident that in a pluralistic polity as that conceived in the Dharmasutras, the cultivators, traders, herdsmen, money-lenders and artisans have authority to lay down rules for their respective classes (*b*). It is not clear whether non-Aryans are included in this enumeration by Gautama; but if they are not, surely the customs of the non-Aryans are referred to when Vasistha(*c*) speaks of laws opposed to those of Aryavarta. Kautilya(*d*) at least declares artisanship to be the profession of the Sudras and it may be presumed that custom was the source of law among the non-Aryans(*e*).

(*a*) Compare Gierke and Maitland's ideas about Group-persons. For functional Groups and Guild Socialism, see Cole's *Social Theory*; for the rights of ecclesiastical Groups see Figgis, *Churches in the Modern State*. The ablest exponent of the Group-theory of sovereignty is Laski.

(*b*) Gautama, XI, 21 (S.B.E. Vol. II).

(*c*) I, 11. (*d*) *Arthasastra* I, 3. (*e*) In later ages this is expressly recognized. Manu mentions Pashanda dharma.

A polity such as has been conceived by the authors of the Dharmasutras leaves almost no room for a king as legislator : he is mainly an executive sovereign ; so much so that he is sometimes depicted as the executor of decisions arrived at by the above-mentioned corporations.

Thus in the Sutra period the king is not the originator(*a*) of any law, (C), (D) or (B). The juridical source of (C) or dharma *par excellence* is ultimately theological but proximately metaphysical ; metaphysical in this sense, that sacred law as such must have a formal Vedic origin. The material source of (C) was the customs of the sistas, while the fundamental features of the sacred law were the theory of Parishad and the fact of agreement. The material source of the (D) department of law was the customs and ordinances made by the corporate bodies(*b*), and the juridical source *seems* to be the corporations themselves. In the (B) department, custom is obviously the material source, while the juridical source is not clear. One thing is common to all these three departments of law : the king's danda is ever ready to enforce law whether it belongs to B, C, or D. The

I,118. Pashandas are for all practical purposes non-Aryans.

(*a*) Duguit maintains (*Law in the Modern State*) that the State is not the creator but the enforcing agent of law. (For the Buddhist-Sangha Buddha was the only law-maker even after his death ; others might expound the laws, but could not make new laws. It reminds us of the sacred law of the Hindus).

(*b*) The guilds had also in the Sutra period some executive and judicial authority. See Ramesh Majumdar, *Corporate Life* etc. pp. 24-25 (2nd edition).

institution of kingship was *sui generis* and the sacred dharma of the king was to enforce even the non-sacred rules comprised under (B) and (D)(*a*).

A query is eminently reasonable here as to why the king of the Dharmasutras is not a law-maker. Apart from the difficulties imposed by the structure of society, the very conception of dharma was such as to preclude the idea of king being a dharma-enacter. Law, if sacred, was eternal, and, if secular, (B, D) was a thing rather of organic growth ; it was expressive of the social culture in its widest sense. Therefore dharma cannot be formulated by the king for the whole society, because then it would be too much mechanical. Law-making by a constituted sovereign can be mechanical and organic at the same time when the form of government is a democracy, and when legislation embraces the whole social life. Therefore, the criticism, that the old codes "mingled up religious, civil and merely moral ordinances"(*b*), is really pointless, because dharma was in olden times co-extensive with the entire life of society. So it is now when the State is every day assuming all sorts of functions. In both these cases, law is a thing of organic growth, a product of national life ; the only difference being that in the one case it is a thing of conscious regulation, in the other it is characterised by a half-conscious process.

The transition from the Sutra period in which law is above the king, to the period represented by the

(*a*) Naresh Sen Gupta, *Sources of Law and Society in Ancient India* p. 92.

(*b*) Maine, *Ancient Law* ch. I.

Arthasastra of Kautilya where the king is the juridical source of all law, is well illustrated by the story heard by Hiuen Tsang about Bimbisara. It is said that in order to prevent fires which had become rather common, Bimbisara passed a law to the effect, that any man in whose house a fire would break out, would be banished. Now it so happened, that one day a fire actually broke out in the palace itself. Bimbisara told his ministers that he would banish himself, because he meant to observe the laws of the country(*a*). This conception of law is transitional in the sense that from the Dharmasutras it borrows the idea that law is above the king, while from the Arthasastra is taken the conception of the king being the juridical source of law.

The Kautilyan description of dharma, vyabahara, charitra and rajasasana as constituting the "four legs of Law" can only be interpreted as illustrating the material sources of law, because in a conflict between rajasasana and the three other sources, the former is to prevail(*b*). Dharmanyaya or nyaya(*c*) in this connection evidently means the equitable reason or simply the reason of the king; and this reason of the king which manifests itself in rajasasana is the juridical source. The Kautilyan conception of law cannot be sacred in its juridical origin because of his

(*a*) Beal, *Buddhist Records of the Western World* Vol. II, Bk. IX pp.165-6; see another story in the same Vol. p. 87.

(*b*) *Arthasastra*, III, 1.

(*c*) Sukra also uses *nyaya* in the same sense. See *Sukraniti* (S. B. H. Vol. 13) IV-V, 106. See *Calcutta Weekly Notes*, Vol. 15 pp. cclxxiv-cclxxvii; ccxci-ccxciv.

political ethics which does not scruple to prostitute religious institutions for purposes of statecraft. Apart from this, there were other factors, external in their nature, which exercised their influence on the Kautilyan conception of law. The agnosticism of the Buddhists did much to destroy the theory of sacred law and its origin, while the *samayas* or resolutions passed by the republican ganas served to bring before Kautilya the real juridical origin of law. Again, the description of some positive laws in the Arthasastra, which have their parallel in Megasthenes, points to the fact that Maurjya kings were law-making sovereigns(*a*). The municipality of Pataliputra was a law-making and a law-enforcing institution(*b*). This realistic environment certainly encouraged Kautilya in the formulation of his theory, wherein rajasasana is depicted as the real juridical source. And of course Kautilya is ever ready with the king's danda to enforce the law for which the sanctions are fines and imprisonment(*c*).

The Kautilyan conception of law as rajasasana or the equitable reason of the king has influenced to a great extent the Manava conception of law. The Manusamhita has been placed by Buhler in the period between the 2nd century B. C. and the 2nd century A. D., while the Arthasastra is a product of the 4th century B. C. Taking into account the fact

(*a*) Some of Asoka's Edicts are clearly of the nature of positive laws (e. g. laws preventing animal slaughter).

(*b*) *Indian Antiquary*, 1905 pp. 51-2.

(*c*) See for example, *Artha* IV, 9. But Willoughby would say that "the ultimate sanction of all law was supposed to be found in the sacred writings". *Nature of the State* p. 12.

that Manusamhita represents an attempt 'to graft a more or less considerable Arthasastra stock upon a slender canonical stem derived from the Dharmasutras,' it will be clear that the Manava conception of law oscillates between the Arthasastric and the Dharmasutraic ones. Or rather it would be truer to say that Manu, following the traditions of the authors of the Dharmasutras conceived law either as sacred or as secular, and ascribed to the latter an origin wholly distinct from that of the former.

After emphasising the divine origin of kingship(*a*) and the need of obedience on the part of the subject, our author immediately(*b*) makes a remarkable contribution to the theory of law, which invests the king with the power of law-making. It says : "Let no man therefore transgress *that law which the king decrees* with respect to his favourites, nor his orders which inflict pain on those in disfavour." This conception of law is typical of the school of Arthasastra, and in a book on Dharmasastra it is remarkable. Probably three factors combined to produce such a conception of law. Of these factors two are realistic, while the third is theoretical, though it is possible that the theory has been largely influenced by, or rather deliberately put forward to explain, certain vital changes in the body politic. The conception of king as lawmaker is not unpalatable when the king is a deity in

(*a*) *Manu* VII, 4-8 ; see also V, 96-97. For a parallel passage see *Sukraniti*, I, 141-3. Sukra mentions the name of Manu in several places of which that at the end of ch. IV is significant.

(*b*) VII, 13 (S.B.E. Vol. 25).

human form and hence should not be despised(*a*). In Manu's time, kingship seems to have been gaining much ground at the expense of the various corporations, and this is why the judicial functions of the king have become so varied and complex. The corporate bodies *viz.* srenis, gramas etc., which got a new lease of life owing to their contact with the Buddhistic *samghas*, were losing their vitality and the king was gradually usurping more and more functions. In such a state of society, to speak of law as being made by the king is not at variance with realities. Again, the Manusamhita represents a stage of Hindu revival against Buddhistic onslaught. Whether it was composed in the time of Pushyamitra or codified at the instance of Samudragupta, the fact is, that the theistic origin of kingship was an anti-Buddhistic doctrine(*b*), and deliberately propounded to arm the Hindu kings with law-making functions and thus to carry on a crusade against the Buddhistic renovations. As the great Asoka had before interfered with Hindu social and religious customs (prohibition of animal sacrifice) by means of rajasasanas, so it would not be wrong if we presume that Manu deliberately made the king a law-making sovereign in order to root out the un-Hindu customs introduced by the Buddhists, with the aid of royal decrees. It was a remarkable innovation, justified no doubt by the exigencies of the times.

But probably Manu was himself taken aback at

(*a*) In England the theory of divine right was developed in its extreme form by Robert Filmer in his *Patriarcha.*

(*b*) In the *Jatakas* kings are held responsible to the people and when occasion demands put to death.

the great demon he has helped to create. He immediately sought to modify his theory, not as Jayaswal has explained, by bringing the king under law(*a*),—this is not modification but nullification—but by conceiving law as composed of sacred and secular law. And herein we see another example of the skilful blending of Arthasastric and Dharmasutraic thought.

In VII, 13, Manu invests the king with law-making functions, but in the immediately following sloka(*b*), dharma is said to be the son and creation of the Lord. This dharma is the sacred law of the Dharmasutras as opposed to the non-sacred law, of which the king is the juridical source(*c*). Thus we get at the conclusion that *dharma par excellence* is attributed to the Lord, while the king is the source of residuary laws(*d*). This is how we can reconcile the two slokas one following the other, and not by taking the latter sloka as superseding and negativing the former one as Jayaswal does. Even in the sphere of sacred law, the origin of which has been attributed to the Lord, it is not clear that the law is supreme, though according to Manu kings are liable to be

(*a*) *Hindu Polity* part II, p. 58.

(*b*) VII, 14 (compare the translations of S. B. E. and Jayaswal, ibid, p. 57).

(*c*) Manu enumerates various sources of law. Obviously they are material sources. I, 118 ; II, 6-18.

(*d*) For a contrary view see Jayaswal, *Hindu Polity* part II, p. 152 where the author says that according to Manu the king could not make new laws. But see Medhatithi's explanation of Manu VII, 13, quoted in footnote S.B.E. Vol. 25, which substantially supports our contention.

fined(*a*). Both dharma (sacred law) and danda(*b*) (power) according to Manu have a divine origin and it has been said that danda in *abstract* is the real king and is also the trustee (prativu) of dharma(*c*). Therefore kingship, looked at from the standpoint of the abstract principle of power, is not subordinate to sacred law, even in the sphere of sacred law, as Jayaswal wants to make out. It is co-ordinate with dharma. In other words, *kings* are subordinate to dharma, but *kingship* i.e. danda, is co-ordinate with and even trustee of *dharma par excellence.*

The origin of Manu's code has a certain resemblance to that of Jewish law; the whole code in its complete form was handed by the Divine Being to Manu, who in his turn asks Bhrigu to recite the code. Thus, in a sense, the whole code has a theological origin.

But there is a popular tradition in India which ascribes all law to an original legislator, a Manu. The interpretation which has been given of this legendary tradition of India by Arabindo Ghose(*d*), is extremely ingenious, and it is difficult to resist the temptation of quoting the relevant passsage. The author says that 'Manu is more a symbol than anything else. His name means man, the mental being. He is the divine legislator, the mental demi-God in

(*a*) VIII, 336.
(*b*) Something like Bodin's *majestas.*
(*c*) VII, 17.
(*d*) *Ideal of Human Unity* p. 227. (This book is extremely suggestive and requires to be more widely known, but the printing, paper and general get-up stand in the way)

humanity who fixes the lines upon which the race or people has to govern its evolution. In the Purana(*a*), he or his sons are said to reign in subtle earths or worlds, or as we may say, they reign in the larger mentality which to us is subconscient and from there have power to determine the lines of development of the conscious life of man. His law is the Manava-dharmasastra, the science of the law of conduct of the mental or human being, and we may think of the law of any human society as being the conscious evolution of the type and lines which its Manu has fixed for it'. Expressed in Stoic terminology, it involves the assumption of an eternal standard of conduct fixed by Brahma, the Universal Reason. To mankind, is declared this law by a Manu, typifying the highest expression of individual reason: the bridge between the ordinary human reason and the Universal Reason being supplied by the proverbial Manu.

From the standpoint of the conception of law, the Rajadharmanusasana section of the Santiparva of the Mahabharat(*b*) probably represents an earlier stratum of thought over which the Arthasastric influence is very negligible. The author first(*c*) gives a vivid and striking description of the nature of danda and speaks about the intimate connection which exists

(*a*) In the *Mahabharat*, *Santi* (R. P.) sec. 67, we find Manu as the first king appointed by Brahma. See also Kaut. *Artha* I, 13.

(*b*) It is placed by some between 4th century B. C. and 4th century A. D.

(*c*) *Santiparva* (R. P.) sec. 121, sl. 8 and after (tr. by P. C. Roy).

between danda and vyabahara and ultimately equates the two. The relation between vyabahara and morality, or in other words, between law and morality, is identical to that of Narayan and his wife Laksmi, for Narayan is danda and hence vyabahara and Laksmi is dharma or morality. In the same chapter, Brahmaic *i. e.* divine origin is attributed to danda.

In this chapter, we get a three-fold classification of vyabahara or law, of which the ultimate origin is divine. The first class deals with ordinary civil and criminal law. Evidence plays a very important part in this class of law where justice is administered and punishment meted out by the king who believes in either of the two litigant parties. This class of law is really Vedic and Brahmaic in origin, though it is the king who enforces these rules. The second class of law is sacred law *par excellence* of which the 'Veda is the soul and the cause'. It includes the rules of morality and the various duties, and these rules of conduct are as binding upon the virtuous people as the ordinary civil and criminal law administered by the dandadhara(*a*). There is a sanction in each of these two kinds of law: a sanction which is relative to the ends in view. The third class of law is connected with family customs, but these customs must be consistent with the sacred Scriptures. All these rules of conduct are productive of good(*b*). It is evident that we again come upon the old classification of law into secular and sacred:

(*a*) *Ibid*, sl. 54.

(*b*) Sls. 50, 54, 55.

the former being equated with the first class and the latter embracing the two other classes. But ultimately there is no distinction between these classes, since the first and last classes converge towards the second(*a*). When we have realised this, we can draw a logical nexus between danda, vyabahara, Veda, rules of morality and lastly righteousness(*b*). The chain of reasoning runs thus: without *danda* there is no *vyabahara*; without vyabahara no *Veda*; without Veda no rules of *morality* and where morality is absent *righteousness* is not possible and consequently the idea of *Brahman* disappears(*c*). The cycle is complete when it is said that Brahman himself, for the protection of the world and for establishing the duties of different individuals, created danda(*d*).

In this rapid survey of early(*e*) Hindu speculations about the nature of law, it must have been noticed that those speculations had been much affected by the theory of *varnasram* on the one hand and by the fact of *pluralism* (viz. economic, social and territorial corporations) coupled with the predominance of *custom and achara* on the other.

(*a*) In one place Bhisma is made to observe that usage or *achara* is the root of all dharma (Quoted by Mandlik in his *Mayukha*, etc. Introduction p. iii) Compare *Yagnabalka* I, 156, *Sacred Books of the Hindus* Vol. 21.

(*b*) Sl. 57. (*c*) *Ibid.* (*d*) Sl. 49.

(*e*) We exclude Yagnabalka, Narada and Sukra, For Narada and Sukra, see my first and last articles.

THE ARTHASASTRA OF KAUTILYA AND THE NITISASTRA OF SUKRA

TREATISES on statecraft, political theories and similar topics were known in ancient Hindu India by the names of *Arthasastra* or *Dandaniti.* Arthasastra literally means the sastra which helps in the acquisition of *artha*, while the term *Dandaniti* means the *niti* or the principles of *danda* or punishment (governance). Kautilya's Arthasastra is the most famous of the Arthasastras known to us. The name of the book itself is Arthasastra, though the term Dandaniti is used by Kautilya ;—once when he classifies the sciences(*a*), and again when he determines the places of Vartta and Dandaniti among sciences and also defines what is Vartta and what is Dandaniti(*b*). In the Santiparva of the Mahabharat, politics is known as Rajadharma, *i.e.*, duties of kings. This subject is also known as Rajaniti(*c*) *i.e.*, rules of governance for the king. Though the Mahabharat treats the subject under the caption Rajadharma, yet the technical term Dandaniti appears in it and the significance of the term is explained in these words. "And because

(*a*) I, 2. (*b*) I, 4.

(*c*) A book by Chandeswara known as *Rajaniti-Ratnakara* has been edited by Jayaswal and has appeared in the *Journal of the Bihar and Orissa Research Society.*

men are led by chastisement, or in other words, chastisement leads or governs everything, therefore will this science be known in the three worlds as Dandaniti(*a*)". In the Mahabharat, Brahma is credited with having originally composed this science, but subsequent abridgments are made by Siva, Indra etc.

Sukracharjya's treatise is known as Nitisastra. By this time treatises on statecraft and similar topics came to be known, not as Arthasastra or Dandaniti, but as Nitisastra. Kamandaka and Sukra who came later than Kautilya wrote their treatises under the title *niti*. There was one Usanas who is credited with having written a treatise on "Dandaniti" and who is said to have held that Dandaniti or Politics is *the* science(*b*)—a saying which reminds us of Aristotle. Now it is held by some that Sukra's treatise is nothing but Usanas' Dandaniti in a revised edition—probably on the ground that Sukra's *nitisastra* is an all-comprehensive vidya(*c*)—"useful to all and in all cases and is the means for the preservation of human society(*d*)."

The categories of thought and the topics dealt with in the Kautilyan Arthasastra and the Sukraniti are more or less the same. We have seen that the term

(*a*) *Mahabharat* (tr. by P. C. Roy), Santi, sec. 59.

(*b*) Kautilya, *Artha.*, I, 2.

(*c*) Lines 8-24 of *Sukraniti*, ch. I (*Sacred Books of the Hindus*, Vol. 13) will make it clear. It is difficult to understand what Winternitz means by saying that "the most important branch of the Arthasastra is politics *which as a separate science is also called Nitisastra.*" Readership Lecture at the Calcutta University, 17th Sept., 1923, *Calcutta Review*, April, 1924.

(*d*) *Ibid.*, lines 8-9.

Dandaniti occurs in the Arthasastra of Kautilya. Likewise in the Nitisastra of Sukra both the terms Arthasastra(*a*) and Dandaniti(*b*) occur. Roughly it seems that the terms Arthasastra, Dandaniti and Nitisastra are more or less convertible terms. In the scheme of classification of sciences which Kautilya accepts, there is no place for Arthasastra as such,—there are Anvikshaki, Trayi, Vartta and Dandaniti and nothing more(*c*). Now a question may be asked as to why should Kautilya choose to designate his treatise as Arthasastra and not as Dandaniti? Kautilya means by Dandaniti, rules (niti) of punishment, *i.e.*, government (danda). And Arthasastra is defined as follows(*d*),—the science which treats of the acquisition and growth of *artha*, *i.e.*, territory is termed Arthasastra. In order to answer the query which we have set to ourselves, it will be better if we first of all care to know what Kautilya meant by Vartta. By Vartta—which Kautilya accepted as one of the four sciences—he meant agriculture, cattle-breeding and trade(*e*). The reason why Kautilya preferred to designate his treatise as Arthasastra is probably this. The scope of Dandaniti seemed too narrow for the purpose of our author ; the scope of Vartta by itself was to a great extent irrelevant to the subject-matter kept in view. But the purpose of our author would be amply served if some parts of Vartta are treated alongside of Dandaniti. It would be clearer if we

(*a*) Sukra, IV-III, 110-1.
(*b*) Sukra, I, 303-4. (*c*) *Artha.*, I, 2.
(*d*) XV, 1.
(*e*) I, 4.

now express ourselves in modern terminology. To Kautilya, Vartta meant Economics, and Dandaniti rules of Government and the art of Politics. Now Kautilya's point of view of Arthasastra is identical to that of *Prince* of Machiavelli, in as much as both the king of Kautilya and the Prince of Machiavelli are actuated by a policy of acquisition and expansion. Now this policy of annexation and land-grabbing implies both political and economic principles, since for a successful policy of expansion, two things are indispensable, *viz.*, a well-filled treasury and an efficient army obtained solely through Vartta(*a*). Because of this, Kautilya's Arthasastra treats Dandaniti in full and Vartta in parts ; or in modern terminology, his treatise deals with *art of politics plus "political" economy.* Hence it is not to be wondered at that the entire second book of the Arthasastra in all its 36 sections deals with economic topics of a political character(*b*).

We have said above that the categories of thought and topics dealt with in the Arthasastra and the Sukraniti are *more or less the same.* They are not identical, since the Sukraniti, though less voluminous than the Arthasastra, is more comprehensive in its outlook and scope. Just as a hypothetical question was put to Kautilya as to why he preferred designating his treatise as Arthasastra, so Sukracharjya might be interrogated about the propriety of his designating his treatise as *Nitisastra* and not as *Dandaniti* or even

(*a*) I, 4.

(*b*) The first and second chapters of Bk. 4 are also economic, the second chapter of Bk. 5 is also of that character.

Arthasastra. Both the terms are to be found in his book. The term Dandaniti occurs where Sukra urges the king to study the traditional four branches of learning(*a*)—the very same scheme of classification of vidyas which we meet with in the Arthasastra. The term Arthasastra also occurs in Sukraniti where Sukra enumerates the primary *vidyas* and primary *kalas*(*b*). But Sukra prefers to designate his treatise as *Nitisastra*, because he wants to make his sastra more comprehensive than Arthasastra and therefore than Dandaniti—in fact, it is social philosophy and sociology in its most comprehensive sense. It is called Nitisastra because it guides and governs—because it sets the standard for human action—be it in social, economic or political sphere. And because it fixes a norm and thereby regulates human action, it is more or less couched in imperative mood. But that does not mean that it is merely an art, because "the propositions which are true of the action of man in his political capacity are also rules for action(*c*),"—and therefore a social vidya— such as nitisastra is—is both a science and art at the same time(*d*). In

(*a*) I, 303-4.

(*b*) IV-III, 110-11—the whole section is devoted to a description of the 32 primary *vidyas* and the 64 primary *kalas*. It is interesting to find in this enumeration that some *kalas* are closely related to their corresponding *vidyas*. Compare the following from Mackenzie's *Manual of Ethics*, p. 11—"The dependence of an art upon its corresponding practical science is of a very much closer character."

(*c*) *Greek Political Theory* (Plato and Prɾd), by Barker, p. 10.

(*d*) Aristotle often expresses himself in the imperative mood and he also emphasises the value of the science of politics as a director of practice, *ibid*, p. 11.

order to prove the superiority of Nitisastra to other sciences, Sukra says that "other sastras treat of certain specialised departments of human activity (and hence can be useful only in limited cases), whereas nitisastra is useful to all and in all cases and is the means for the preservation of human society(*a*)," and again, "nitisastra conduces to the desires and interests of all and hence is respected and followed by all. It is also indispensable to the prince, since he is the lord of all men and things(*b*)." This last quotation proves that nitisastra is not merely a political vidya, but a social vidya as well Thus it deals with the *art of politics, political economy and economics* and *social ethics*—under the last term being included general rules of morality(*c*) and various household duties(*d*).

Dandaniti is logically prior to Vartta or other vidyas because the cultivation of all other vidyas is made possible only when there is a *danda-dhara*; none the less, the scope of Dandaniti is narrower than that of Arthasastra, while the scope of the latter is again narrower than that of Nitisastra(*e*).

(*a*) Sukra, I, 8-9.

(*b*) *Ibid*, lines 23-24.

(*c*) Chap. III deals with this.

(*d*) Part of ch. IV sec. 4.

(*e*) *Cf.* "The field covered by the *Spirit of Laws* (Montesquieu) is so extensive as to make it a work rather of social science than of politics proper." Dunning—*Political Theories from Luther to Montesquieu*, p. 394. Aristotelian conception of politics is similar. 'Hence social Philosophy was for Plato almost the same thing as politics and hardly distinguishable from ethics and the theory of education.' *Outlines of Soc. Phil.* by Mackenzie, p. 22. *Garuda Purana* makes Arthasastra a branch of Nitisastra. (Quoted Ghoshal)

The first book of Kautilya opens with a classification and definition of sciences and the place of Dandaniti therein. Then he goes on to speak about royal discipline which to all Hindu writers on politics is very important(*a*). Sukra also insists on discipline for the king. The importance of this moral discipline for the king—who is looked upon both by Kautilya and Sukra as the mainspring of the entire political mechanism—cannot be overestimated, specially so when the king is the maker of the age(*b*). Sukra begins his book by emphasising the synthetic, comprehensive and the utilitarian aspect(*c*) of the nitisastra and then passes on to the most important category of his sastra, *viz.*, kingship. Sukra does not give the classification of the various vidyas and kalas in the beginning of his book, but reserves it for a later section, where he briefly describes the special characteristics of each. In dealing with moral discipline for the king one thing is to be particularly noticed in both Kautilya and Sukra. After emphasising the supreme importance of the restraint of the organs of sense to the king, both Kautilya and Sukra give actual instances of kings coming to grief through their failure to provide discipline for themselves(*d*). This is something of a historical method, but to be frank, the method here

(*a*) See Shamasastri, *Evolution of Indian Polity*, Preface xiv.

(*b*) This idea is to be found also in *Santiparva* in explanation of the 4 epochs—*Satya, Treta, Dwapar* and *Kali*.

(*c*) I, 4-9.

(*d*) Kautilya, I, 6 ; Sukra, I, 135-6, 137-8, 225-6, 287-90.

is historical, rather in appearance, than in reality. Thus the Kautilyan and Sukraic appeals to Ramayana Mahabharat and Puranas are made rather for the purpose of sustaining, than for the purpose of discovering, rules of discipline for the king(*a*).

Any one who goes through the two treatises may not unreasonably complain as to why so much importance has been given to the category of kingship, even though both the writers accept the theory of *saptanga*, *i.e.*, the theory of the State as an organism of seven limbs. The saptanga or organismic theory is defective in that the most important organ in this seven-limbed organism—the people—is conspicuous by its absence(*b*). Had there been this organ, then there would have been two "rival" directing organs. As it is, the category of kingship absorbs the major portion of the canvas.

Both Sukra and Kautilya accept the theory of saptanga(*c*). Had our authors been dominated by a mechanical, as opposed to an organic, conception of the State, probably the category of people would have loomed large. But in an organic conception of the State, there is but one directing organ and that is the

(*a*) Compare the following from the *Introduction* by Tozer to Rousseau's *Social Contract*, p. 40—"—and Rousseau's meagre and inaccurate historical knowledge is used, not to furnish materials for inference, but to illustrate preconceived ideas or foregone conclusions." On this point *viz.*, historical method, see also Dunning's observations on Machiavelli's method in his *Political Theories*.

(*b*) Even if the concept *rastra* or *janapada* be taken to mean "people," still they have not got that emphasis which they deserve.

(*c*) The theory as presented by them enumerates the constituent elements of the State.

brain; and if the category "people" is ignored by our authors in the theory of saptanga, the way is clear for the king to be in sole charge of the directing organ. Probably this is the reason why Sukra compares the king of the saptanga to the human head(*a*). There is another reason why the category of kingship is so important. To Sukra nitisastra is the most important of all the sciences and arts, because without niti the stability of no man's affair can be maintained(*b*); to Kautilya the course of the progress of the world depends on the science of Dandaniti(*c*). Moreover, both Sukra and Kautilya in their treatises presuppose a social structure known as *varnasram*. The duties relevant to *varnas* and *asrams* are thought to be eternal, and it is the duty of the king to see that the various *varnas* keep within their respective duties(*d*). Logically therefore kingship comes first of all; because it is only through fear of punishment meted out by the king, each man gets into the habit of following his *swadharma* or duty. Without the *danda* and the *danda-dhara* there is no mine and thine, everything is chaos and confusion. Therefore kingly duties are regarded as the foremost(*e*) and hence kingship is the most important category.

(*a*) I, 123-4; also Kautilya says, "the king and his kingdom are the primary elements of the state," VIII, 2.

(*b*) I, 20-22.

(*c*) I, 4. (*d*) *Artha*, I, 3, Sukraniti I, 45-47.

(*e*) Compare, "kingly duties *first* flowed from the original gods." "The eternal duties (of man) had all suffered destruction. It was by the exercise of Khattriya duties that they were revived." *Santiparva*, sec. LXIV, also—"The Brahmachari, the householder, the recluse in the forests and the religious mendicant—all these walk in their

This stress on the concept of kingship may be explained in another way. Both the Nitisastra and the Arthasastra—the latter in particular—are written from the standpoint of the governor and not governed. The philosophy of both is a study of the art of government, rather than a theory of state. Their field is *Politik* and not *Staatlehre* as Dunning would say. They do not enquire about the origin of the state—they do not bother their heads as to what should be the proper relation between the sovereign and the subjects—they do not discuss about the nature of rights. Both 'are interested in the establishment and operations of the machinery of government—in the forces through which governmental power is generated and applied'. Of course Sukra's scope is much wider than that of Kautilya, and he every now and then treats us to general rules of morality(*a*) and social customs and institutions(*b*) which are non-political in their nature. But nonetheless it is Sukra who emphatically declares along with the author of the Santiparva that the king is the maker of the age. The central theme of the Arthasastra in particular and of Nitisastra to some extent is the successful creation of big empires by kings. In fact, Sukra goes so far as to declare that 'conversion of princes into tributary chiefs is one of his eight functions'(*c*) and

respective ways through fear of chastisement." *Santiparva* sec. XV.

(*a*) After finishing the third chapter Sukra says, "the nitisastra that is common to the king and the common people has been narrated in brief."

(*b*) IV-IV.

(*c*) I, 245-8.

feels no scruple in saying that kings who cannot make other princes pay tribute are oxen, *i.e.*, fools(*a*). In both the authors the central thought is the '*methods* of those who wield the power of the state, rather than the fundamental relationships in which the essence of the state consists'. Closely related to the point which we are just now discussing, *viz.*, that the treatises and the Arthasastra in particular, were written from the standpoint of the governing class—is the point, and important too, that Kautilya's Arthasastra was in the nature of a practical manual of statecraft and administration for the king(*b*). Sukra's nitisastra is the outcome of a series of lectures by the learned professor to his disciples, the *Asuras*, on the essence of *niti*—political, social and economic no doubt; but it is patent to any and every reader of Sukra that almost the entire book is devoted to political *niti* and that again from the standpoint of the king. In fact, the first and second chapters are entirely political—being devoted to an enumeration of and discussion about the duties and functions of the king

(*a*) *Ibid*, lines 249-50.

(*b*) Compare—"There is always this practical bent in Greek political thought. The treatises in which it issues are meant, like Machiavelli's *Prince*, as manuals for the statesman. Particularly is this the case with Plato. True to the mind of his master Socrates, he ever made it the aim of his knowledge, that it should issue in action, and he even attempted to translate his philosophy into action himself, and to induce Dionysius to realise the hopes of the *Republic*. Nor shall we do justice to Aristotle unless we remember that the *Politics* also is meant to guide the legislator and statesman, and to help them either to make, or to improve, or at any rate to preserve the states with which they have to deal."—Barker—*Greek Political Theory*, p. 10.

and other state officials. The third chapter deals with general rules of morality no doubt, but those rules are meant both for the king and the common folk(*a*) and hence they acquire a political interest. All the other chapters and sections—with the exception of the third section in chapter four and portions of the next section—are entirely political and written as a sort of manual for the king(*b*).

The point that the Arthasastra was written as a manual of the art of government(*c*) receives added justification from the fact that its author was the celebrated Chanakya(*d*)—the famous Brahmin minister of Chandragupta Maurjya. Just as the *Prince* of Machiavelli was written when Italy was divided into a number of petty states and Machiavelli, pained at heart, beseeched Lorenzo to place himself at the head of a united Italy by following the rules set forth in the *Prince*, so the Arthasastra of Chanakya was

(*a*) III, 652-53.

(*b*) So also Bossuet the French bishop-courtier was commanded by Louis XIV to undertake the education of the Dauphin and the result was a political treatise for the use of his pupil.

(*c*) Compare the following from Machiavelli's *Prince* (translated by Marriot) in the beginning of the 15th chapter —"It remains now to see what ought to be rules of conduct for a prince towards subject and friends." Machiavelli's *Prince* was written with the object of indicating the *methods* by which Lorenzo Di Piero De Medici (to whom the book was dedicated) can make himself the master of entire Italy.

(*d*) Kautilya is the gotra name, this name occurs at the end of every chapter—see the footnote in Jayaswal's *Hindu Polity*, part I, p. 4. See also Shamasastri's *Introduction* to the Arthasastra (Eng. tran.)—Winternitz is of opinion that the Arthasastra is the work of a Pundit—not of a statesman. *Calcutta Review*, p. 16, April 1924.

composed as a practical manual for his royal disciple, Chandragupta(*a*),—till then a petty monarch. The rules are relevant for the government of a small kingdom surrounded by friendly and hostile kingdoms and the pen-picture drawn by the author certainly points to the conclusion that Chandragupta has not as yet acquired that paramount power which he was subsequently destined to enjoy(*b*).

The Arthasastra and the Nitisastra do not profess to be theories of state, and hence no systematic account is to be found about the origin of the state. In one place (*c*) the origin of kingship and hence that of the state is said to be the result of popular election(*d*)—the people preferring to pay the king in the shape of taxes in return for protection from *matsyanyaya*, *i. e.*, anarchy. But evidently this is not the opinion of Kautilya, because the relevant passage is put in the mouth of one spy replying to another. As regards the origin of kingship, Sukra says that the ruler has been created by *Brahma* a *servant* of the people getting his revenue as remuneration. Here the origin of the

(*a*) "The name of Chandragupta or of any other person, however celebrated he might be, has no logical connection with a literary work meant to be of universal application. It is a painful truth that Indian writers cared more for logic than for history." Shamasastri's article in the *Calcutta Review*, April, 1925.

(*b*) Vincent Smith (*Early History of India*, 3rd Edition, p. 137) says—"we may accept it (the Arthasastra) as an authoritative account of political and social conditions in the Gangetic plain in the age of Alexander the Great, 325 B.C."

(*c*) *Artha*, I, 13.

(*d*) Both the *Mahabharat* and the *Dighanikaya* contain such accounts.

institution of kingship is placed at the door of Brahma. How can we explain this silence in Kautilya and the short explanation of Sukra as regards the origin of the state or for the matter of that, the origin of kingship? The explanation lies in the fact that to both Kautilya and Sukra the state is a natural institution—natural in the sense that it exists from the very dawn of *varnasram* or Hindu society. Since the state is ingrained in the human nature, it needs no explanation as to its origin historically. The fact that the ruler has been made by Brahma (as Sukra says), means that the institution of kingship and hence that of state exists from the beginning. Sukraic conception of the ends and aims of the state is essentially secular, and this theological explanation of its origin is not really theological(*a*) but to emphasise the fact that rudiments of political control are to be met with in the very dawn of history(*b*).

Just as the origin of life is shrouded in mystery, so, the origin of the state has up till now eluded the search of political theorists, sociologists and anthropologists. Modern scientists can at best explain the origin of this by that, or they can resolve a compound into its constituent elements, but they will have to

(*a*) This theological origin loses much of its theological character when in the very same breath Sukra makes the king 'a servant of the people.' Again, the fact is to be noted that Sukra makes a distinction between a good and a bad king—the former being a *nara-devata.* Also hints at deposition are given in some places and king's right to respect is based on personal merit and not on birth. See I, 363-4.

(*b*) Recent researches in savage life tend to confirm this statement.

postulate the existence of a first cause; otherwise they will tend to move in a circle. Probably this is the reason why the institution of kingship in its rudimentary form has been laid at Brahma's door by our author,—meaning thereby, that the state or the king is one of the first creations of Brahma, the creator(*a*).

From another standpoint the concept of kingship is one of those postulates of thought without which everything is confusion. Virtue, progress, duty, morality and religion are all dependent on the institution of kingship. The establishment of *varnasram-dharma* can be thought of only when there is a king, because "through fear of punishment meted out by the king, each man gets into the habit of following his own *dharma*(*b*)." 'The subjects become virtuous, do not commit aggressions, and do not speak untruths only because there is the king to wield the rod of punishment. Even the cruel become mild, the wicked give up wickedness, even beasts become subdued, the thieves get frightened, the garrulous become dumb, the enemies are terrified and become tributaries, and others are demoralised(*c*).' And last of all *danda* or rather the *danda-dhara* is the foundation

(*a*) "Among the Greeks the state was considered as an institution existing in itself and of itself and as determined by the very nature of things. As such it had a divine origin, as did all things in the phenomenal world." Willoughby, *Nature of the State*, p. 43; also—'the conception of the state as natural and therefore indirectly divine,' *ibid*, p. 44.

(*b*) *Sukra*, I, 45-7; for a similar idea see *Arthasastra*, end of I, 4.

(*c*) *Sukra*, IV-I, 92-8; for a similar idea see *Santiparva*, sec. 15.

or stay of virtues(*a*). Thus we come to the conclusion that the very conception of human society—not to speak of social progress(*b*)—is impossible without the first postulate of kingship. The logical contradictory of the state is anarchy, *i.e.*, *pralaya*.

Reference has just been made to the fact that to both Kauṭilya and Sukra the state is a natural institution. By the term "natural" it should not be understood that the evolution of the state and the consequences and results thereof are of natural growth, *i.e.*, human effort has nothing to do with it. Far from it. It is said by Sukra(*c*) that "the king is the cause of the setting on foot of the customs, usages and movements and hence is the cause or maker of time (*i.e.*, the creator of epochs)" and again "the king is the cause of the prosperity of this world(*d*)," and "the faults are to be ascribed neither to the age, nor to the subjects, but to the king(*e*)." Kautilya also says that the progress of the world depends on Dandaniti(*f*). Now this is an intensely modern conception. The doctrine that the future is not in the lap of gods but is amenable to human control, that man can control his own destiny(*g*), that there is no such thing as Fate—all these things are clearly put forward as preliminaries to the proposition

(*a*) *Sukra, ibid*, 101-2.
(*b*) *Artha*, I, 4.
(*c*) I, 43-4.
(*d*) I, 127-28.
(*e*) IV-I, 116-7.
(*f*) I, 4.
(*g*) *Sukra*, I, 73-4.

that the king is the maker of the age(*a*). What is popularly known as *daiva* or Fate is nothing but the work of man in previous births. Kautilya seems to assume all these propositions and indirectly sets forth the doctrine of *puruskara* when in a remarkable passage (IX, 4), he says that wealth passes away from an idiot who consults the stars too much, for wealth is the star of wealth and the stars in the sky have nothing to do with it and that capable men will certainly secure wealth even after a hundred attempts. Now this conception of politics coupled with the doctrine of the "open future" comes with natural grace from both Kautilya and Sukra. Kautilya by his own exertions helped Chandragupta to found an extensive empire by overthrowing the Nanda dynasty(*b*). Sukra is the preceptor of *Asuras*, the traditional enemies of the gods, and hence he cannot possibly be accused of any sympathy with Daiva or Fate(*c*).

With this emphasis on the doctrine of *puruskara* we may naturally pass on to the category of kingship—since it is the king who is *paurusa* personified and

(*a*) With these principles before us the theological background in *Sukraniti* (origin of kingship) fades away.

(*b*) This fact is mentioned by Kautilya at the end of his book. See *Kamandaka* XIV,21.

(*c*) *Artha*, VI, I, 257. This apotheosis of *paurusa* or human effort is sufficient to meet the charges of some writers who would stigmatize Hindu political thought as theological and metaphysical—for in Sukra the ruler is *paurusa* personified, since in him lies tho power to create a *Satya* or a *Kali Yuga*. On this point see Benoy Sarkar's *Pos. Background of Hindu Sociology*, Bk. II, part I pp. 31-2. See *Ind. Historical Quarterly* Vol. I, No. 3, p. 559.

who by wielding the *danda* helps the *puruskara* or creative intelligence of man to manifest itself.

Both Kautilya and Sukra proceed on the assumption that sovereignty necessarily belongs to kings; they never stop to discuss the comparative merits of monarchy, aristocracy or democracy. Kautilya at least was cognisant of the possibility of democratic forms of government when he says that sovereignty may be the property of a clan(*a*); but more than that is to be met with in the Arthasastra when we refer to the eleventh Book where the names of some republics are mentioned which had existence in history(*b*). The treatment of the subject of *gana* is exceedingly scanty—the subject is treated not by itself, but as an incident in the foreign policy of the *vijigisu* king. Though the comparative merits of the different forms of government are not discussed by Kautilya, yet he concedes that the "corporation of clans is invincible in its nature and being free from the calamities of anarchy can have a permanent existence on earth(*c*)." No doubt both Kautilya and Sukra treat of monarchy as the emblem of sovereignty; but that does not mean that there are no checks to the exercise of royal power(*d*). Both the treatises assume ministry as

(*a*) I, 17. Shamasastri in a footnote to the English Translation says—"A clear proof of the existence of republican or oligarchical forms of Government in ancient India'—a clear proof of the existence of confusion between theorizing and fact.

(*b*) A detailed treatment of this subject is to be found in Jayaswal's *Hindu Polity* and Majumdar's *Corporate Life* etc.

(*c*) I, 17.

(*d*) On this subject see the writer's article on *Checks to Tyranny* etc.

an essential adjunct to the system of monarchy propounded by Kautilya and Sukra. The *raison-d'etre* of ministry is that a 'single wheel can never move(*a*).' Other checks to autocracy may be found in the established duties of the four *varnas* and the four *asrams* and also in the local customs of the country—however obnoxious they might seem. The king is not the creator of *varna-dharma* and *asram-dharma*—he merely upholds the observance thereof. Even Kautilya and Sukra—however radically secular they might appear—cannot avoid making the socio-religious institution of *varnasram* an essential substructure in their plan of treatment. People following such obnoxious customs as eating beef, marrying the widows of their brothers are not to be condemned by the king(*b*),—a definite hint about the supremacy of customs. Both Kautilya and Sukra do not like Narada(*c*) or Calvin(*d*) say that oppressive and worthless kings are to be obeyed without a murmur; hints are given by Kautilya that impoverished and disaffected subjects voluntarily destroy their own master(*e*). Sukra cannot tolerate a king who does not listen to the counsels of his ministers(*f*)—to him an autocratic king is a 'thief in the form of a ruler.'

(*a*) *Artha*, I. 7 ; see also *Sukra*, II, 1-8. For a fuller treatment see R. G. Basak's article in the *Indian Historical Quarterly* 1925 Vol. I, Nos. 3-4.

(*b*) *Sukra*, IV-V, 94-101.

(*c*) S. B. E., XVIII, 22.

(*d*) *Calvin's* Institutes, Bk. IV, ch. XX, para., 25. See Dunning, *Pol. Theories* (From Luther), p. 29.

(*e*) *Artha*, VII, 5 ; I, 10 ; VI, 1.

(*f*) II, 515-16.

Other hints at deposition are given in some more places(*a*).

The point to be noticed in this connection is that neither Kautilya nor Sukra invests the subjects with any *right* to depose or kill a tyrant. Students of politics familiar with the *Vindiciae contra Tyrannos* or Buchanan's *On the Sovereign Power among the Scots*(*b*) or with the Spanish Jesuit Mariana's advocacy of tyrannicide will be surprised not to find, either in Kautilya or in Sukra, any theory about the rights of the people. The explanation is three-fold. Firstly, both the books are written—and the Arthasastra in particular—from the standpoint of the governor and not the governed. Therefore the 'governed' class do not fall within the scope of the books and as such the treatment of the so-called rights, or for the matter of that, duties of the subjects, is dispensed with. Secondly, neither Kautilya nor Sukra pretends to expound a theory of the State. Had our authors first of all set to themselves the task of formulating a resonable theory of the State—the first problem for which they would have been seeking a solution would have been the problem of king *vs.* subjects. Free self-determination of action is an essential attribute of man(*c*)—but how are we to harmonize this fact with another fact—*viz.*, the subjection of human

(*a*) I, 277-8, 279-80; II, 5-8; IV-VII, 826-29.

(*b*) See Dunning, *Pol. Theories* (From Luther).

(*c*) We may recall here Sukra's doctrine of *puruskara*. It is this theory which establishes freedom of will and makes man a 'moral' being by holding him and none else responsible for his actions.

groups to a coercive control by a king— the *governor*. When discussing this universal problem, our authors would have discussed whether any actual or theoretical limit should have been placed upon the powers of the king in enforcing his will—for otherwise why should free self-determining beings acquiesce in being coerced. In other words, they would have discussed the problem of right—natural or legal,—in all its aspects. Lastly, the outlook of Hindu writers on Arthasastra, Nitisastra and so on is swayed by the theory of *swadharma*(*a*). It means that every man in society has a group of duties—special to his *position*. To the Hindus the phenomenon of social order is the resultant of duties. Hence the problem of the rights of the people has not been treated directly, but indirectly the same objective has almost been gained by enumerating the duties of the kings. In fact, this is why politics in the *Santiparva* is known as *raja-dharma*. Rights and duties are nothing but the same thing looked at from two opposite points of view(*b*). Thus the right of a citizen not to pay oppressive taxes can be converted

(*a*) This theory of *swadharma* is to be found in Plato's *Republic* where three distinct classes with separate duties are assumed in his ideal state. Bradley also speaks of *swadharma* and argues "that fulfilment of *station* is a good enough practical canon of morality." Barker, *Pol. Thought from Spencer*, p. 65. (Compare the Hindu saying—Death in the performance of one's own duty or *dharma* is preferable to a mode of life where one has to perform duties which should be performed by others). Something of the same nature is implied by Bosanquet when he speaks of "Position." (*Philosophical Theory of the State*, ch. 8, pp. 205-7) And kingship is a high "Position" or "Station".

(*b*) For a discussion about the nature of rights and obligations see Bosanquet, *Phil. Theory of the State*, ch. 8.

into the duty of a king not to tax his subjects over-much. And the Hindu writer on politics—be it secular or theological—prefers to put his statements in the garb of duties(*a*).

We have just now seen that the concept of rights has not been attained either by Kautilya or by Sukra, but none the less their idea of kingship is not an unfettered tyranny—and this is possible because of their, and more especially of Sukra's, emphasis on duty(*b*).

Advocates of the theory of divine origin of kings might find an ally in Sukra, merely on the basis of some texts in the first chapter(*c*). In one place it is said that "the king is made by Brahma, a servant of the people" and in another connection it is put forward that the king has been made out of the "permanent elements of Indra, Vayu, Yama, Sun, Fire, Varuna, Moon and Kuvera." Our contention is, that the divine origin as put forward by Sukra is seemingly divine, and in substantiating our case we

(*a*) 'The fact remains that in the political thought of Greece the notion of the individual is not prominent, and the *conception of rights seems hardly to have been attained.*" Barker, *Greek Pol. Theory*, p. 7 ; see also Wilde's *Ethical Basis of the State*, pp. 213-14, where the *duty* of free speech is emphasised and also the quotation from Plato's *Apology*, 31.

(*b*) "It is unimportant in theory whether a system of law starts with a consideration of rights or of duties."—Holland, *Jurisprudence*, p. 88. In early Roman law the idea of duty was much more prominent than that of right. Till 1868 the Japanese seem to have possessed no word for legal right. See the footnote in Holland's *Jurisprudence* p. 86.

(*c*) Lines 141-3, 375.

give the following five arguments. Firstly, the texts should be read as part of the whole treatise which is predominantly positive and secular. Secondly, the statement, that the king has been made by Brahma, a servant of the people, means, as explained beforehand, that the origin of kingship is co-eval with creation and hence can be laid at Brahma's door. Moreover, if divine origin should be thought of, it passes our comprehension why the former statement should be watered down by the following statement, *viz.*, servant of the people(*a*). Thirdly, the statement about the king being made out of the permanent elements of the eight gods is merely metaphorical and is nothing but a catalogue of the functions and duties of the kings conveniently and metaphorically expressed so as to appeal to the popular imagination(*b*).

Fourthly, if the theory of divine origin be accepted, we fail to see why Sukra should be so insistent on drawing a distinction between good and bad kings and should say that a virtuous king is a part of the gods, while a king who is otherwise is a part of the demons(*c*). Not content with saying this, he threatens such a king with the condition of lower

(*a*) Here again the concept of duty is prominent. This *service* to the people consists in protection which is his primary duty. Sovereignty is not a right to be claimed because of divine origin, but a matter of duty imposed by Brahma (if we accept Brahmaic origin). This will be evident if we refer to line 375, ch. I.

(*b*) This will be explained later on when we deal with the functions and duties of the king and the state.

(*c*) I, 139-40.

animals(*a*) or hell(*b*) and kings with divine origin going to hell, well—that is an incongruity, to say the least of it. Lastly, the threat of deposition(*c*) to kings who are oppressive, points to the fact that kingship is a human and not a divine institution. That kingship is not divine, is further evident from the fact that when an oppressive king has been expelled, "in his place for the maintenance of the state, the priest with the consent of the *Prakriti* should instal one who belongs to his family and qualified(*d*)". Kautilya also assumes the human origin of kingship as will be evident if we refer to the chapter(*e*) where purity or impurity in the character of ministers is tested by various kinds of temptations.

Thus though the king in Sukra and Kautilya is a human being, yet no harder and more exacting life can be conceived of than that of a ruler. Both Kautilya(*f*) and Sukra(*g*) have been, in this respect, dominated by the most exacting standard and they have drawn up detailed time-tables of work for the king(*h*).

While dealing with this point, it should be noticed

(*a*) I, 64-8.

(*b*) I, 63; 171.

(*c*) The threat of deposition is not clothed in the garb of a *right* of the people but the relevant statements are expressed as matters of fact.

(*d*) II, 551-2.

(*e*) I, 10.

(*f*) I, 19.

(*g*) I, 551-69.

(*h*) Yagnabalka also has got a similar exacting time-table.

that both Sukra and Kautilya have not cared to distinguish private duties from public duties. It is possible that in the eyes of both the king is always a public person: whatever he does has got a public interest; or it might be interpreted as a legacy of the rajadharma school of politics.

From this, we may pass on to discuss the duties and functions of the king and the state. The public functions or duties of the king are also the duties and functions of the state, since the king is the "head" or the brain of the state. The functions of the king have been very succinctly and beautifully described by Sukra in some passages(*a*) which have been referred to in connection with the so-called divine origin of kingship. We have just now seen that the king, according to Sukra, is made out of the permanent elements of eight gods. This is but another way of saying that the functions of the king represent the sum-total of the distinctive functions of the eight gods, *viz.* Indra, Vayu, Yama, Sun, Fire, Varuna, Moon and Kuvera. Indra represents the kingly function of *protection* of person and property. The god of air (Vayu) helps in the diffusion of scents: so the king may be of great help in the *diffusion of culture*(*b*) and

(*a*) I, 141-61; *cf.* Manu, VII, 4; *Santiparva,* sec. 68, sl. 41-7.

(*b*) In I, 767, Sukra says that *Pandits,* females and creepers do not flourish without resting grounds,—which means that the state must actively encourage learning. Again in I, 155, the king is said to be able to endow his subjects with good qualities. In I, 741, Sukra says that "the king should always take such steps as may advance the arts and sciences of the country". See also I, 740, also IV-VII 53-8.

thus is the "generator of good and evil actions". "As Yama is the god who punishes (human beings after death) so also the monarch is the *punisher* of offences (in this world)(*a*)". Again as the sun-god dispels darkness and creates light, so the king destroys irreligion and is the *founder of religion*. The functions of Fire (Agni) and water-god (Varuna) are probably complementary and both represent economic functions, *i.e.*, functions connected with wealth. "Like Agni, the prince is the purifier and enjoyer of all gifts(*b*)"—probably this stands for the *tax-realising* functions of the king. The other function represented by Varuna, is, as we have said, complementary, because with the realised taxes he conducts the government and thus maintains everybody. This is the *tax-spending* function of the sovereign for the welfare of the subjects. The distinctive function of Moon is to please human beings. Needless to say this is not a real function at all. Sukra unnecessarily repeats the function of protection, when Kuvera is laid under contribution in the making of a king. Probably this repetition is an indication of the anxious emphasis which Sukra wants to lay on the function of protection which is the primary duty of the king and without which we revert to a condition of *matsyanyaya*(*c*).

(*a*) *Ibid*, line 147.

(*b*) *Ibid*, line 148.

(*c*) A beautiful description of the condition of *matsyanyaya* or anarchy is given in the Santiparva—which in some essentials resembles that of Hobbes. In this pre-political state—as depicted in the Santiparva—there is no mine and thine, no morality, no rules for marriage and no property; in fact chaos reigns all round.

These functions have been modified by Sukra himself here and there. In one place, the king is said to possess the attributes of father, mother, preceptor, brother, friend, Kuvera and Yama(*a*). In another place, eight functions of the king have been enumerated, *viz.*, "punishment of the wicked, *charity*, protection of the subjects, performance of Rajasuya and other sacrifices, equitable realisation of revenues, *conversion of princes into tributary chiefs*, quelling of the enemies and *extraction of wealth from land*(*b*). It will be seen, that in this case too, the king has got *eight* functions(*c*), though in the former case, there are really six functions.

Taking all these functions together and ignoring those which are mere repetitions, we may say that there are *nine functions* of the king according to Sukra. These are the functions of protection and punishment(*d*), tax-realising and tax-spending functions, wealth-producing functions, functions as regards the advancement of learning and religion, and functions of charity(*e*) and conquest.

Kautilya does not in so many words speak of the functions of the king in a compact passage, but from a careful study of his treatise we can say that he

(*a*) I, 155-60.
(*b*) I, 245-48.
(*c*) The other case is where the king is said to be made out of *eight* gods.

(*d*) These two functions may be combined into one and thus there may be *eight* functions; but it is better to keep them separate—protection having reference to external enemies and punishment to miscreants within the state.

(*e*) In modern language it means the responsibility of the state for the helpless, weak and poor.

attributes to the king at least seven out of the nine functions described by Sukra. The two functions which he leaves out of account refer to promotion of education and religion. From one passage it may be inferred that the king is to look after the interests of religion, because there the king is asked to "personally attend to the business of gods, of heretics, of Brahmans learned in the Vedas, of cattle, of sacred places(*a*)" and so on. But from a study of the whole book it will be evident that Kautilya looked upon religion as a convenient intrument of state policy and did not hesitate to prostitute religious institutions for political purposes(*b*). Education finds no place in this catalogue, obviously, because of the fact, that the Kautilyan king is throughout dominated by one ideal, *viz.*, expansion.

The essential functions of the king, *viz.*, protection and punishment are referred to by Kautilya in the chapter(*c*) where he defines Dandaniti. The two other functions, *viz.*, realisation of taxes and spending of taxes, which are no less essential than the other two just mentioned, are also spoken of by Kautilya in the chapter(*d*) where the business of collection of revenue by the collector-general is described. The three other functions, which are non-essential, are the functions of charity and general welfare. wealth-

(*a*) I, 19.

(*b*) XIII, 1.

(*c*) I, 4.

(*d*) II, 6. In this chapter the various sources of revenue (*durga, rashtra, khani, setu, vana, vraja* and *vanik-patha*) and the various heads of expenditure are described.

producing function(*a*), and lastly, the function of conquest. Many of the modern paternal and socialistic functions of the state have been anticipated by Kautilya, when he lays it down, that "the king shall provide the orphans, the aged, the infirm, the afflicted and the helpless with maintenance. He shall also provide subsistence to helpless women when they are carrying, and also to the children they give birth to(*b*)". In abnormal times, *i.e.*, in times of famine, "the king shall show favour to his people by providing them with seeds and provision(*c*)". In case this proves insufficient, the "policy of thinning the rich by exacting excessive revenue, or causing them to vomit their accumulated wealth may be resorted to(*d*).' The economic functions of the state, as described by Kautilya, are numerous and important too, and indicate in a forcible way the materialistic bias of the Arthasastra(*e*). The king, or for the matter of that, the state of Kautilya, is to "carry on mining operations and manufactures, exploit timber and elephant forests, offer facilities for cattle-breeding and commerce, construct roads for traffic both by land and water, and set up market towns(*f*)." Not content with this brief catalogue of economic functions, Kautilya devotes

(*a*) Function of causing immigration or emigration is also referred to in II, 1.

(*b*) II, 1. (*c*) IV, 3.

(*d*) *Ibid.* In modern technical language, this is the principle of progressive taxation carried to its logical extreme. Compare *Sukraniti*, IV-II, 17-23.

(*e*) In fact, the name Arthasastra itself suggests materialistic leanings. *Artha* is wealth or earth.

(*f*) II, 1.

the second book of his Arthasastra almost entirely to a description of the functions and duties of the various State Superintendents, who are put in charge of agriculture, pasture-lands, forest-produce, mining and manufacture, commerce, weaving, etc.(*a*). But Sukra "does not probably think of any state-conducted enterprise(*b*)" in industry or commerce, though extraction of wealth from land(*c*) is one of the functions of the state of Sukra.

Among the functions of state, the function of conquest is a non-essential one ; but viewing it from the standpoint of both Kautilya and Sukra, it would seem to be an essential function. This is evident from the fact that kings who cannot attain to the status of *samrat* or *sarvabhauma* are spoken of in a discourteous tone by Sukra(*d*). Again, though Sukraniti is *not merely* a treatise about statecraft, yet a fourth part of the book is devoted to topics connected with the subject of conquest(*e*). That Sukra regarded war as a natural phenomenon, is evident when he

(*a*) For a lucid account of all these things, refer to Narendra N. Law's *Studies in Ancient Hindu Polity.*

(*b*) *Pos. Background of Hindu Sociology,* Bk. II, part 1, by Prof. Benoy K. Sarkar.

(*c*) *Sukra,* I, 245-8. But Prof. Benoy K. Sarkar expresses surprise (see *Pos. Background,* p. 119) that "we do not have indications of *ager-publicus, domaine* or crown-land" in *Sukraniti.*

(*d*) I, 249-50.

(*e*) IV-VI, IV-VII—The latter section deals with foreign policy and is full of details about horses and elephants—so necessary for war. This love for details is also found in the *Politics* of Aristotle, *e.g.,* music. Kamandaka devotes two-thirds of his treatise to foreign policy and conquest.

enjoys one characteristic feature—to him the whole world is bound. The conqueror-king of Kautilya has vassal-kings under him, whose land he must not covet for fear of causing provocation to the *circle of states.* The conqueror-king of Kautilya represents a dynamic ideal, the static ideal is reached by a *chaturanto-raja*(*a*). Just as in the mediaeval Europe, an ambitious ruler would aspire to the status of the Byzantine Emperor, and Charlemagne was a faithful follower of the ideal of universal sovereignty,—so the typical king of the Nitisastra and the Arthasastra, and of the latter in particular, would not find a stable equilibrium, until he is the sole monarch "up to the very ends uninterrupted(*b*)."

From their idealizing the conception of universal sovereignty, it follows as a logical corollary, that neither Kautilya nor Sukra can conceive of states independent of each other, enjoying what is called "Renaissance Sovereignty". After the mediaeval political ideals had faded away, there appeared on the European canvas certain states independent of each other and each enjoying established government; and political theorists began to adjust their theories to the changed environment. The theory, which they then formulated and which served as a mirror of the political conditions of Europe of that age, cannot be an adequate interpretation of the characteristic features of the modern state—in fact the modern state is not economically or

(*a*) Machiavelli's static ideal would be well represented by a king of *United Italy* only.

(*b*) Fichte is of opinion that expansion is the *dharma* of every civilised state and universal monarchy the goal.

politically independent of other states(*a*). The vacuum which existed between independent states, and which resulted in constant fighting, was sought to be filled up by the Law of Nature and International law(*b*). International law as a solution of the inter-statal problem has not proved a success. We might imagine that both Kautilya and Sukra with the help of *a priori* method discussed that the political equilibrium sought to be achieved among a group of states in a state of *matsyanyaya* with each other, will be of an extremely unstable character(*c*)—however much the modern states may pay lip-service to rules of international morality. Both Kautilya and Sukra—and the latter in particular(*d*)—are of opinion that man never does his duty unless threatened by the *danda* of the king(*e*). If this be their estimate of man, a moral being, what more can we expect of states possessing no conscience like man and obeying no common superior. And thus the concept of *sarva-bhauma* fits in well with their estimate of human nature(*f*) and the assumption of a condition of matsy-anyaya among different states.

(*a*) In this connection see the essay "The State and Society" in the *Theory of the State, Bedford Lectures*, and also pp. 173-4 in *Recent Developments in European Thought*, edited by Marvin.

(*b*) Maine, *Ancient Law*, ch. IV.

(*c*) Dante points out that "the world was never quiet except under the monarch Augustus Caesar" and hence seeks to prove that the principle of unity is essential. See D. Burns, *Pol. Ideals*, p. 108.

(*d*) IV-I, 92-98.

(*e*) *Cf. Manu*, VII, 22.

(*f*) Of course unity need not be under *one ruler*, but Kautilya and Sukra could not conceive of that—a world-federation.

The function of conquest is one of the many functions of the Sukraic king no doubt, but it would be truer to say that the main proposition of the Arthasastra is aggrandizement, pure and simple. Hence, the more the emphasis on the doctrine of aggrandizement, the less is the respect for religion and morality. The Nitisastra does not separate politics from ethics so much as the Arthasastra does—as a matter of fact, the Nitisastra is *not merely* political, but is a system of morals, social, political and economic.

Kautilya has been severely taken to task by Bana, the author of Kadambari for his espousing the cause of pernicious political ethics in the following words: "Is there anything that is righteous for those for whom the science of Kautilya, merciless in its precepts, rich in cruelty, is an authority; whose teachers are priests, habitually hard-hearted with practice of witchcraft; to whom ministers, always inclined to deceive others, are councillors; whose desire is always for the goddess of wealth that has been cast away by thousands of kings; who are devoted to the application of destructive sciences; and to whom brothers, affectionate with natural cordial love, are fit victims to be murdered(*a*)." Bana is both right and wrong in his estimate of Kautilya and his Arthasastra. Had Bana been careful in distinguishing between the standards of public and private morality, he would not have been so "merciless" in his criticism

(*a*) Preface X, of the English translation of Arthasastra (Shamasastri).

of the Arthasastra(*a*). The Kautilyan king in his private life is an ideal king, because "with his organs of sense under his control, he shall keep away from hurting the women and property of others, avoid not only lustfulness, even in dream, but also falsehood, haughtiness, and evil proclivities ; and keep away from unrighteous and uneconomical transactions(*b*)" ; but when the "good" of the state requires it, he must be prepared to practise treachery, deceit, hypocrisy and sacrilege, if need be. Thus, in order to get rid of a courtier, who is dangerous to the safety of the kingdom, and who cannot be put down in open daylight, a spy is sent out by the king to instigate the brother of the seditious minister and to take him to the king for an interview. The king promises to confer upon him the property of his brother and causes him to murder the minister, and when he has killed his brother, he is also put to death then and there as a fratricide(*c*).

Again in the next chapter(*d*), the king, if in need of filling up his treasury, may set up a temple with an idol erected during the night, and taking advantage of the religious credulity of his subjects, he may thus collect money, or by another device, the king may get rid of a seditious person and at the same time replenish his treasury. A quarrel is got up

(*a*) Bana is right in this sense that the Kautilyan king would never shrink from using the most obnoxious means in order to gain his political objective.

(*b*) Artha., I, 7.

(*c*) V, 1. This chapter recounts similar measures against seditious persons.

(*d*) V, 2.

between the members of a seditious family, and poisoners previously engaged may administer poison to one of them. The other party is accused of the offence and their property confiscated(*a*). Or again, a spy, under the garb of a physician, may declare a healthy person of seditious character to be unhealthy, and under the pretext of administering drugs, he may administer poison(*b*). Thus we see, that for the revenue and safety of the kingdom, no measure is too mean to be employed. Kautilya "did not at all deny the excellence of the moral virtues, but he refused to consider them as essential to, or conditions of, the political virtues." Kautilya's "political man is as entirely dissociated from all standards of conduct save success in the establishment and extension of governmental power, as is the 'economic man' of the orthodox school from all save success in the creation of wealth(*c*)." The first principle in Kautilya's Arthasastra is the safety of the State, and to this end, the dictates of morality are subordinated. This moral indifferentism to problems of politics, which has paved the way for the complete separation of politics from the apron-strings of ethics, has earned for him as much odium as Machiavelli has to bear by being called

(*a*) *Ibid.*

(*b*) *Ibid*—for the filling up of treasury the Superintendent of Religious Institutions may collect the property of the gods and carry that to the king's treasury. Something like confiscation of *Devottar* property.

(*c*) The above two sentences within quotation marks refer to Machiavelli, but the author might have written them in connection with Kautilya.

"Machiavellian(*a*)". Yet the Kautilyan king is not immoral in his private life. We might say that Kautilya is not immoral, but unmoral in his politics.

The same thing may be said about his attitude towards religion. Kautilya himself is an orthodox Brahmin, and the Kautilyan king is to receive daily benedictions from sacrificial priests, and is to salute both a cow with its calf and a bull by circumambulating them, and also to personally attend to the business of gods, of heretics, of Brahmins learned in the Vedas, of cattle and of sacred places. But when the "good" of the state requires it, he will not hesitate to prostitute religious institutions for political expediencies. This will be evident from an instance just given, *viz.*, setting up an idol during the night for replenishment of the treasury. We might say that Kautilya is not irreligious, but unreligious in his politics(*b*).

This moral and religious indifferentism of Kautilya is seen in all its hideousness, when we view the Kautilyan king from the standpoint of a warrior. For conquering an enemy, poisoners and prostitutes(*c*) are freely recommended. For killing an enemy king, when he visits a place of worship for purposes of

(*a*) *Kautilya* literally means "Duplicity Personified". The name *Chanakya* stands for unscrupulous statecraft and diplomacy.

(*b*) Machiavelli viewed religious sentiment as an important instrument of state policy.

(*c*) Compare Louis XIV's policy towards the Stuart kings of England; *Artha.* XI, 1; XII, 2; Manu also recommends wholesale poisoning of foodstuffs, forage and water. See *Manusamhita*, VII, 195.

worship or pilgrimage, various devices are recommended in minute detail(*a*). Again, in order to infuse enthusiastic spirit among his own men and frighten his enemy's people, the Kautilyan king may give publicity to his power of omniscience and his power of holding intercourse with the gods(*b*). Needless to say, these are magical tricks(*c*) and abuse of religious institutions.

Sukra has not been able to completely free politics from ethics—in fact, his conception of Nitisastra as a comprehensive system of morals stands in his way. The Nitisastra mainly enumerates various kinds of *duties*, while the Arthasastra enumerates the *methods* by which a king may aggrandize himself; It is significant in this connection that Sukra nowhere mentions Kautilya, but he mentions Manu in several places(*d*). The political virtues in the Nitisastra are almost conditioned by moral virtues, though in the sphere of foreign relations and of warfare, he sometimes follows Kautilya, though at a respectful distance. Sukra has also got a spy-system, but it is not for nefarious purposes: it is used by the king for the purpose of knowing as to who among his subjects are accusing his

(*a*) Thus weapons are kept inside an idol. See XII, 5.

(*b*) XIII, 1. Spies are concealed in the interior of hollow images, and they speak to the king. The next chapter deals with the sinister methods by which an enemy-king can be got under power.

(*c*) Besides magical tricks, there are some chapters on witchcraft. (*Artha.*, Bk. XIV). Witchcraft is, properly speaking, a part of the art of war. See Hopkins' article in the *Journal of the American Oriental Society*, 1889, p. 31[illegible].

(*d*) I, 418-19; ibid. 387-8, 395-6, 397-8, 400-1, 409-10, 411-12, 413-14.

conduct and for what, so that he might get rid of his faults(*a*). In one passage, the Sukraic king is advised to collect funds by hook or by crook(*b*), but in the next breath the king is threatened with the destruction of his kingdom if he collects funds by forsaking morality(*c*). The fact is that Sukra has always an uneasy conscience whenever his king tries to subordinate morality to politics. That Sukra has not been able to distinguish clearly between the standards of public and private morality, is evident from the passage, where our author is unable to explain why robbery and bloodshed should be excusable in kings, while they are condemnable in ordinary robbers(*d*). He can only explain it by assuming that morality is relative. Had he pushed to the logical extreme this line of thought, he could have found out, that what is immoral in an individual, is not necessarily so in a king who is acting on behalf of the state. Sukra is nowhere an advocate of absolute morality(*e*), but it is curious, that the Sukraic king does not employ those sinister methods at least in internal politics. In external politics, for the purpose of overpowering the enemy, Sukra, like Kautilya, advo-

(*a*) I, 260-65.

(*b*) IV-II, 3-4.

(*c*) *Ibid*, 15-16.

(*d*) Sukra. V, 65-72 ;—compare "Alexander the Great and the Robber-chieftain."

(*e*) Because in Sukra's philosophy there is room for wine, gambling, anger, sensuousness and cupidity. See also IV-VII, 664-67, where the Brahmins are advised to take up arms to kill the wicked Khattriyas. See V, 62-73.

cates the use of prostitutes and dancers(*a*). He seems not to condemn telling lies on the part of a king like Srikrishna(*b*), and even advocates the use of "blockade" in warfare(*c*). He also appreciates the effectiveness of warfare conducted against the dictates of morality, and as a proof of this, quotes the well-known incidents of Rama *vs.* Bali, Krishna *vs.* Yavana and Indra *vs.* Namuchi(*d*). Notwithstanding all these, he cannot help enumerating some rules, which apply to warfares conducted according to the dictates of morality(*e*)—and here he appears before us as an ardent follower of Manu, who prohibits the use of hidden weapons, and barbed, poisoned or burning arrows(*f*). In matters of internal politics, Sukra seems to be dominated by moral judgments, while in those of external affairs, politics and ethics seem to dominate each other, his emphatic enunciation of the theory of relativity of virtues and vices notwithstanding(*g*).

We have seen that Sukra has not been able to free politics from ethics, though in one or two places

(*a*) V, 31-3.

(*b*) V, 118-9.

(*c*) IV-VII, 740-1. Compare *Manusaṁhita*, VII, 195, 196.

(*d*) IV-VII, 725-27—an example of historical method.

(*e*) *Ibid*, 716-24—*cf.* the rules of modern warfare.

(*f*) Manu, VII, 90, 91, 92, 93. These sutras of Manu contradict sutras 195, 196 of the same chapter.

(*g*) V, 70-72—see Mackenzie's *Manual of Ethics*, pp. 354-7. While on this point of relativity, it is interesting to learn as Adam Smith remarks (*Theory of Moral Sentiments*, part V, sec. II) that "in the reign of Charles II, a degree of licentiousness was deemed the characteristic of a liberal education". See footnote I, *Manual of Ethics*, p, 356; compare Sukra, I, 215-16. Compare the *ethos* of the educated community of Bengal in the early 19th century.

he tries to do so. His conception of law illustrates this attitude very clearly. Sukra has got a clear conception of what Holland calls 'positive law.' In a passage, Sukra says that "the following laws are to be always promulgated by the king," and then goes on to enumerate the various laws which the king should announce by beat of drums and by placards and posters. In the event of disobedience to these laws, adequate punishment is meted out to the offenders(*a*). Thus we see, that the Sukraic king is a law-making sovereign. But—and here the influence of ethics and sacred literature comes in—the king is always to decide cases according to the dictates of the Dharmasastras(*b*), so much so, that the king commits a sin if he administers the secular interests otherwise than in accordance with the spirit of the Dharmasastras(*c*). Again, any one can have a retrial, if he pleads that the decision of the king is against dharma(*d*). In another place, it is said, that the king should administer *Smriti* in the morning and *nyaya* in the noon(*e*). Again, one of the essential requisites in the administration of justice is *Smritisastra*(*f*), and to crown all, a court of justice has been defined as "a place where the study of the

(*a*) I, 587-626.

(*b*) IV-V, 9-11, 18-9, 22, 83-4.

(*c*) IV-V, 535-6.

(*d*) *Ibid*, 549-50.

(*e*) *Ibid*, 106,—"Nyaya" means king-made laws. Can it mean Equity? See *Calcutta Weekly Notes* Vol. 15, pp. cclxxiv-cclxxvii.

(*f*) *Ibid*, 72-3.

social, economic and political interests of men takes place according to the dictates of the Dharmasastras(*a*).' Here we find the Sukraic king, not a law-making sovereign, but a law-administering sovereign. Now then the question is, who makes the law? The answer to this, according to Sukra, would probably be this. There is the law or dharma uncreated: rules of conduct for the various castes and orders according to this dharma are set down by the sages in their Dharmasastras(*b*). The king is there to administer this law as declared by the sages(*c*). He may promulgate fresh laws, but they must not supersede the sastras, and the new laws must have their basic principles rooted in dharma. So far it is clear, but who is to see whether the king-made laws are or are not in accordance with dharma? To this, Sukra furnishes no clear answer; but it is to be presumed that in a conflict between the king-made law and the dharma, the former is to go to the wall: since the application of the law is in the hands of judges well-versed in the Dharmasastras(*d*).

Kautilyan conception of law is in keeping with

(*a*) *Ibid*, 83-4.

(*b*) Compare the Stoic idea of the Law of Nature and the modern 'intuitionist' philosophy.

(*c*) We are to resort to the intuition of the sages, probably because their reason is not depraved. So Aristotle says: "To invest the law then with authority is, it seems, to invest God and intelligence only".—*Politics*, p. 154 (tr. by Welldon)

(*d*) IV-V, 23-28, 40, 50-51. But Sukraic king is advised not to tamper with time-honoured customs even though they contradict the sastras. This is nothing but a counsel of expedience. See IV-V, 94-101.

his conception of politics freed from the trammels of sacred literature. In his Arthasastra, he distinguishes four kinds of law, viz. *dharma* (sacred law), *vyabahara* (evidence), *charitra* (custom) and *raja-sasana* (edicts of kings); and the king is advised to administer justice according to these four kinds of law. Should there be any conflict between *charitra* and *dharma* or between *vyabahara* and *dharma*, then the matter shall be settled in accordance with sacred law; but "whenever sacred law is in conflict with rational law (king's law), then reason shall be held authoritative; for there the original text (on which the sacred law has been based) is not available(*a*)." It is but reasonable to assume that Kautilya, who does not scruple to abuse religious institutions for purposes of statecraft, should bestow on the king-made law a status superior to that of sacred law. But it is in theory only, because the Kautilyan king is mainly a law-administering sovereign(*b*), as will be evident from the fact, that the Kautilyan king is advised to

(*a*) Artha. III. 1 (Shamasastri). Evidently the reason of the king is implied.

(*b*) No Hindu writer can get over the fact that there are certain caste duties which are eternal. Jayaswal says, (*Hindu Polity* part II, p. 152) 'He could make new laws according to the Arthasastra, according to Manu, he could not do so; but when he could make laws, he passed only regulatory laws and not laws substantive or laws making him arbitrary." But the Sukraic positive laws are not *regulatory* laws.

In this connection, it is interesting to note that Asoka was mainly a law-making sovereign. The regulations formulated in the Second Minor Rock Edict, and specially those relating to the protection of animal life, were rigorously enforced, and thus the liberty of the Hindus in this matter was seriously curtailed.

maintain the world in accordance with the injunctions of the triple-Vedas, wherein the duties of the four *varnas* and the four *asrams* are defined(*a*), and also because of the fact, that for the administration of justice three members acquainted with sacred law and three ministers are required(*b*). However, in all this, we get a glimpse of the distinction between the formal and the material sources of law.

In concluding this study, we might point out that both Sukra and Kautilya conceived of the state as a corporate body, as will be evident from their theory of *saptanga*, but that neither of them, properly speaking, had any theory of the state. Both, and Kautilya in particular, were dominated by the category of kingship. Both viewed the state as a means, which neither created rights(*c*), nor created duties(*d*), but created *order*. The individual was *generally*(*e*) left to realise his own self in this order created by the *danda* of the king. The state or political organization was a necessity to the individual, because otherwise, the three aims of life, *viz.*, *dharma*, *artha*, and *kama* (*trivargas*) could not be attained ; or, in other words, there could be no morality, no property and no family-life without the state(*f*).

(*a*) I, 3.
(*b*) III, 1.
(*c*) They had no conception of rights.
(*d*) Most of these duties are eternal and defined in the sastras.
(*e*) In Arthasastra, in some spheres, the state-action was comprehensive.
(*f*) Kautilya is dominated by materialism, *i.e.*, by *artha* ; see I, 7. Sukra's philosophy is more synthetic : he seeks to harmonize *dharma*, *artha*, *kama* and *moksa* ; see III, 2-5.